163256

A Memoir of Resistance

163256

A Memoir of Resistance

Wilfrid Laurier University Press

WLU

We acknowledge the support of the Canada Council for the Arts for our publishing program. We acknowledge the financial support of the Government of Canada through the Book Publishing Industry Development Program for our publishing activities.

Library and Archives Canada Cataloguing in Publication

Englishman, Michael, 1921–
    163256 : a memoir of resistance / Michael Englishman.

(Life writing series)
ISBN 978-1-55458-009-5

1. Englishman, Michael, 1921–. 2. Jews—Netherlands—Biography. 3. Holocaust, Jewish (1939–1945)—Personal narratives. 4. Holocaust survivors—Canada—Biography. I. Title. II. Title: One six three two five six. III. Series.

DS135.N6E56 2007   940.53'18092   C2007-901768-1

Cover design by Angela Moody, Moving Images. Cover image (lower) © iStockphoto.com/ Brett Laxton. Text design by Catharine Bonas-Taylor.

Every reasonable effort has been made to acquire permission for copyright material used in this text, and to acknowledge all such indebtedness accurately. Any errors and omissions called to the publisher's attention will be corrected in future printings.

This book is printed on Ancient Forest Friendly paper (100% post-consumer recycled).

Printed in Canada

Published by Wilfrid Laurier University Press
Waterloo, Ontario, Canada
www.wlupress.wlu.ca

Dedicated to the memory of
my family who perished in the Holocaust,
and to my children, grandchildren, and great-grandchildren

CONTENTS

Preface / ix

Introduction / xi

1 Growing Up Jewish in Amsterdam / 1

2 Deportation / 14

3 From the Burght to Vught—and Auschwitz / 26

4 The Coal Mines of Janina and the Buna Works / 31

5 The Death March to Dora-Nordhausen and
Building the "Secret Weapon" / 41

6 Liberation / 50

7 Finding the Children / 54

8 Picking Up the Pieces / 63

9 Canada, Here We Come! / 68

10 Déjà Vu / 73

11 Fighting Back by Telling the Truth / 81

12 Family Reunion / 91

13 March of the Living—April 2004 / 98

Afterword / 105

Appendices / 107
I *Family Relationships*
II *List of Prisons and Concentration Camps*

THERE IS NO WAY TO PROPERLY DESCRIBE THE HORRORS OF THE NAZI CON-centration camps. Even after all these years much of what I saw and experienced is difficult for me to talk about. But genocide—the mass murder of human beings because of their race or religion—continues to happen long after the defeat of the Nazis. I have come to realize that speaking out about what happened to the Jews in Europe from 1933 to 1945 is the only way I can help to prevent similar acts of brutality in the future.

I started speaking to students and community groups about Hitler's "war against the Jews" in 1985. I was shocked to learn how little my audiences knew about the barbaric treatment of prisoners in the Nazi concentration camps. The Nazis and their cohorts excelled at inflicting the greatest possible psychological and physical pain on other human beings, and the camp commanders and guards were so proud of how well they did their jobs that they took photographs of their atrocities and mailed them home to their families. But the Nazis' wholesale slaughter of innocent people did not begin with the concentration camps or with the gas chambers; it began with words.

How was it that the nightmare of the Holocaust came out of a country that had been a shining example of European democracy, a country that has produced an astonishing number of the world's greatest composers, writers, artists, and philosophers? It happened because after the German people had elected Adolf Hitler and his Nazi party, the fascists' first priority was to destroy the democracy that had allowed them to flourish. Hitler took full advantage of his democratic right to freedom of speech and used it to eliminate the democratic rights of others, especially of Jews and opponents of his regime. He used the media—radio and newspapers—to spread his hatred for Jews and anyone who was not Aryan and blame them for Germany's economic and political problems. He convinced Germans that if they could get rid of all those non-Aryans, Germany would rule the world. One of the most important lessons Hitler has taught us is that freedom of speech without any restrictions can be deadly. It's like driving a car with no brakes.

I have written this book so that young people can learn the truth about what happened to the Jews and know not to ever take anything in society for granted. Racism begins in small, subtle—even ordinary, seemingly harmless—ways, but it is a poison to any civilized society. If young people speak out loudly and clearly against racism and hatred, they can help to ensure that the horrors of the Holocaust never happen again. Crimes committed in the name of religion are still crimes. In fact, preaching the destruction of human beings in the name of any religion is the greatest crime against religion itself.

—Michael Englishman

Words at the Ready

MARLENE KADAR

MICHAEL ENGLISHMAN'S STORY OF RESISTANCE IS A MODEST ACCOUNT OF bravery and heroism in a time of tremendous anguish. The time of resistance is the time of the Holocaust; and although the environment shifts, Englishman's roots are in The Netherlands, and in Amsterdam in particular, where Dutch Jewry were very active in the underground movements to free Holland and end Hitler's hold on its peoples. There are too few memoirs about the Holocaust in Holland, and even fewer autobiographies or testimonies by Dutch Canadians who immigrated to Canada after the war, and fewer still by writers who would call themselves Jewish Dutch Canadians.[1] Englishman's memoir is a welcome contribution to our understanding of the Holocaust in The Netherlands, and is a testament to one man's journey through that period in modern war and genocide history that evokes what Dan Bar-On referred to in 1999 as "the indescribable and the undiscussable."[2] In *163256: A Memoir of Resistance*, Englishman describes and discusses what cannot easily or even directly be remembered or spoken.

Englishman's memories of youth are clearly depicted and seem quite ordinary on the surface: the narrator was athletic and played many sports, he went to a Jewish Day School, he struggled in school because he was left-handed, and he was devoted to his home and his family life. The tragedy is that not one member of this young man's family survived the Holocaust years.

Like many youth, Englishman developed close friendships as he matured into adulthood, and equally as a prisoner in Hitler's camps. What astonishes readers is that Michael Englishman remained true to his dear friend, Max Pels, even after the torment, even while he nursed his own wounds, even after losing all he had known as home before Auschwitz. This book revolves around a promise: Michael never forgot his promise to Pels, a memorable promise, a gracious promise, one that also likely ensured Michael's survival after the war.

This promise is tied to friendship and loyalty, two concepts that would in great measure determine who #163256 would become, and how his life would continue after his incarcerations in two prisons and five concentrations camps. Englishman survived numerous beatings and other methods of torture, starvations, and extreme mental anguish; he speaks on many occasions of the dire feeling of utter loneliness engendered by his experiences, a feeling that finally begins to fade when he begins a new family. The circumstances under which he builds this new family are a testament to the quality of his friendships and his promise. They also underline his sense of loyalty and his perseverance, and within and between his words, a quiet need to have faith in the goodness of his people. This quiet need permeates the memoir and brings both sadness and joy to the various short tales that interrupt the larger narrative of suffering and overcoming, of regeneration, of immigration and new life. Michael's tale about his new family and how it came to be is a near-mythic story, and yet in his eyes it is all so ordinary, just the way things turned out.

Michael Englishman's sister Esther was related to Max and Rika Pels' family by marriage. The Pels family lived across the road from Michael's wife-to-be, Henrietta [Yetty], and they had two children, Katy and Philip. Michael explains and in so doing foreshadows that "Yetty and I became close friends with the Pels family. We knew their children ... from the time they were born" (13). Most important to this particular narrative is the fact that Michael had long been a close friend of Rika Pels' brother, Aaron, so the connections between the Pels and the Englishmans ran deep and long.

Michael and Yettie's parents and siblings, and other family members, were rounded up for deportation in August 1942, just after Yettie and Michael were married (for names and dates, see the Appendices). During these horrific round-ups, or razzias, Max and Rika Pels would hide their children in Michael and Yettie's basement "between two piles of coal" (23). Because Jewish children were most vulnerable during a razzia, the Pels parents eventually reasoned that their own children must be sent away in order to increase their chances of survival (24). The Dutch underground arranged for Katy and Philip to be taken to a rural area in the southern part of Holland to live with a Catholic farm family, and Max and Rika went into hiding on their own. They did not know where their children had been taken. It is during the narration of this story that Michael reveals the promise: "Max Pels and I had made a pact to look after each other's family" (24). If Max and Rika did not return to Amsterdam after the war, then Michael would try to find the children and look after them. Max, too, promised that if Michael did not return, he would look after Yettie. A year later, Yettie, Rika, and Michael were arrested and taken away. Yettie and Michael were eventually taken to the Vught concentration camp in Holland, and later separated en route to Auschwitz-Birkenau. Rika changed her identity and pretended she was a prostitute; she was sent away from Amsterdam but not to the Dutch concentration camp at Vught.

Michael heard nothing more about her until the end of the war. Apparently she and Max had been arrested in Amsterdam in 1944 and transported to Auschwitz-Birkenau where Max is thought to have perished. Rika, however, was sent to a slave labour camp in Willishtal and Sarvenstein to work in a munitions factory. She was moved again, this time to the camp at Theresienstadt, where she was liberated in 1945. Other survivors confirmed that both Yettie and Max had perished, and as Michael writes, the fact that Michael and Rika were the only survivors in their families brought them closer together.

When the end of the war came, Michael and Rika were reunited. Michael returned to his "house" only to find no living family members and no home to return to. He writes: "I had experienced my most devastating moment of utter loneliness when I came back to Amsterdam and sat on the steps of the Biermasz laboratory across the street from the house where I had lived. The house I was no longer allowed to enter" (61). It is at this point, broken and lonely, Michael sets out to find Katy and Philip—as he promised Max and Rika he would do. His promise saves him from total despair.

After a period of adjustment that most of us would find difficult to imagine, the promise is fulfilled and the remaining members of these two families merge. "Hendrika Pels and Michel Engelschman" were married in 1949 and established a home in Amsterdam until the children, Katy and Philip, were ready to join them full-time. In the spring of 1952, they made the choice to leave The Netherlands for Canada with their two children. Michael writes that "looking after my new family left me no time to dwell on my own pain" (61) and observes that it is not until he witnessed his new family doing "everyday things" that his feelings of utter loneliness begin to fade.

As difficult as the act of remembering trauma is for those who suffer it first-hand, Michael Englishman writes his memoir in the present time, a time of remembering and reliving the anguish, as a man with new strengths and new resolve. The words that describe these events and feelings are also the words that give Michael back his history and his memories. As he says in the Preface, "the Nazis' wholesale slaughter of innocent people did not begin with the concentration camps or with the gas chambers; it began with words" (ix). Although Michael Englishman does not dwell on his own pain, he admits that "the horrors of the concentration camps and the grief of losing my parents, my sisters, my wife, were and still are, always with me" (61). The grief is already always there. Michael Englishman is already always #163256. In spite of these two inescapable truths, Englishman tells his stories with humour, and all of them with his beloved Rika, Katy, Philip, and his grandchildren, close to his heart. The two worlds of horror and love coexist in this narration as they are rarely able to do in Holocaust narratives. Englishman is a vociferous advocate of using words to "speak out loudly and clearly against racism and hatred" (x); he understands words as actions. This memoir is an action, an act of remembering and witnessing, but also a political act, a cautionary tale directed at all of us, but primarily at the young whose responsibility the world will inevitably become.

It is for young people that Michael Englishman has written this book. He wants to warn them that nothing in the social world can be taken for granted. Words must always be at the ready, to say and do the right thing.

NOTES

1 Wilfrid Laurier University Press published one of the first memoirs of wartime Holland: Henry G. Schogt, *The Curtain: Witness and Memory in Wartime Holland*, Life Writing Series (Waterloo: WLUP, 2003). A self-published book appeared in the 1990s [n.d.], Gerard Van Dykhof's *The Way It Was: Untold Stories of the 1940s and the Dutch Resistance*, but it did not enjoy wide circulation. The book focuses on the heroic underground resistance movement, as almost all WWII stories about Holland do. Although both memoirs are narrated by Dutch Canadians, and give a realistic impression of the hardships the Dutch suffered in Amsterdam and elsewhere during the war, neither author is Jewish. Schogt narrates his family's difficult circumstances as "righteous Gentiles." Also in print is a short autobiographical piece by a Dutch Canadian who is Jewish, Robert Krell. Like Englishman's children, Krell was a very young person in Nazi-occupied Holland, and was reunited with his family only after three years in hiding. See "Confronting Despair: the Holocaust Survivor's Struggle with Ordinary Life and Ordinary

Death" in *Canadian Medical Association Journal* (15 September 1997), 741–744. Thank you to Pana Bountis, Violetta Damm, and Emily S. Young for their assistance.

2 Dan Bar-On, *The Indescribable and the Undiscussable: Reconstructing Human Discourse After Trauma* (Budapest: Central European University Press, 1999).

CHAPTER ONE

Growing Up Jewish in Amsterdam

IN THE SPRING OF 1940, I LIVED AT THE PLANTAGE MUIDERGRACHT 63, Amsterdam, with my parents, Levi, fifty-six years old, my mother Rachel, fifty-seven years old, and three of my four sisters. My father was an accountant and my two older sisters were teachers. Anna, who was twenty-nine, taught kindergarten and Duifje, twenty-three, taught languages: Hebrew, the language of Israel, as well as German, French, and English. Duifje was also deeply involved with the Zionist movement. She was in charge of preparing groups of boys and girls for life on the kibbutzim in Israel. My younger sister, Hendrika, was fifteen. Esther, the eldest, was married to Jacob Buytekant and had a son, Joseph, five years old. I was nineteen years old, a certified electrician, and was attending a technical college for more specialized training. I also had a diploma in bookkeeping, but I wasn't suited to a job where I had to sit still for long periods of time. I was very athletic and boxed, wrestled, played soccer, and swam practically every day.

As a young boy I went to a Jewish day school; I had a difficult time in school because I was left-handed. It was the teachers' duty to convert me and make me a right-handed "normal" child! I resented the pressure that was put upon me. Remember, the teachers were always right ... right?

Starting in grade one, we received special teaching about the Orthodox Jewish religion. When I was in grade six I was nearly thrown out of school because I asked whether it would be possible to teach us something about other major religions too! Was I out of line?

My family lived in the top floor of this house before the war

I was about seventeen years old when I needed surgery on my abdomen to treat a double hernia. The surgeon told my parents that for the rest of my life I should not do any form of manual labour or sports. My father gave me a job in his office. I lasted about three weeks; that's all I could take. Without the approval of my family, I had started to swim again. I was a member of a special trained swimming team called Amsterdam's Redding Brigade (A.R.B.). This team rescued victims inside cars that were under water in the canals in Amsterdam.

In my school days, "racism" was a strange word in Holland—I was simply unaware of it. My friend Ado and I grew up together. I never noticed that his skin colour was different from mine. I was as welcome in his house as he was in ours.

About 140,000 Jews lived in Holland at the beginning of the war, and over half of them lived in Amsterdam's thriving Jewish community. There had been a strong Jewish presence in the Netherlands since the end of the fifteenth century when the Jews were expelled from Spain and Portugal. They had been accepted into Dutch society because of their expertise in trade and finance. The Netherlands was at its height as a colonial power and maritime trading empire. Amsterdam became a world market for diamonds, and the diamond industry that developed into a central part of Holland's economy was run mostly by Jews.

When Jews first settled in Holland, Jewish religious services were held secretly in private homes. But around 1640, the first openly held service was celebrated in a Sephardic synagogue that became known as the "Portuguese synagogue," which Rembrandt immortalized in 1560. It was built on wooden pillars that stood in the water underneath the structure. The pillars are regularly inspected from a small boat. The wooden floor was covered by a thin layer of sand. I was told after the war that several Jewish people had hidden under this wooden floor. During the war, the synagogue was declared international property and off limits to police and army.

The synagogue still stands, although it now houses a museum. The neighbourhood around the synagogue soon became the heart of Amsterdam's Jewish District, with a Jewish market on Sundays and a rich cultural life full of Jewish art and theatre, as well as a bustling street life. I remember the street peddlers with their pushcarts full of all kinds of foods and flowers and other goods. On Fridays, the organ grinder came to play his organ and collect pennies rolled in pieces of newspaper that the people threw out their windows. In Amsterdam's Jewish District, Orthodox and secular Jews lived and worked side by side, and on Saturday afternoons, the Kalver Straat was a meeting place for many Jewish people.

I grew up in the middle of this vibrant community. My family was close. We had our share of disagreements, but there was always room for give and take. I don't remember my father ever raising his voice to us. One wonderful memory of the way he resolved a disagreement that was causing considerable tension in our house has stayed with me. My sister Duifje, whose name means "dove," was a leading figure in the Zionist movement in Holland. She prepared groups of young students who were interested in working on a kibbutz in Israel. She placed them with farmers who were willing to teach them how to grow food and fruit. When the students were able and ready, Duifje would arrange to transport them on a ship to Israel. Father strongly disapproved of Duifje's involvement with the Zionists. He was not a religious zealot, but he was Orthodox in his beliefs and practices. According to him, it was written that only the Messiah, not the Zionists, could bring the Jews back to Israel. Duifje repeatedly tried to explain to Father that the Zionists wanted to prepare the land of Israel for the return of the Jews, with or without the Messiah, but it was to no avail. And to make matters worse, I also became involved in the Zionist movement.

Remember that I am speaking of a time when people believed that parents were always right and that children should be seen and not heard. Children did not openly contradict their parents and parents rarely, if ever, said to a child, "I'm sorry, I was wrong."

Nonetheless, one Saturday morning in the midst of this family struggle, my father and I returned from shul for the Sabbath luncheon. The meal began as it always did with Father saying the blessing over the bread. After we had finished eating, we got ready to sing the opening part of the "Shir Hamaalot," the grace that follows the meal. The song's traditional melody goes back many years, and we all knew it well. On this particular Sabbath, however, my father suddenly started singing the words of the "Shir Hamaalot" to the melody of "Hatikvah," the national anthem of Israel. To make the words fit the melody properly, he must have rehearsed it many times. Can you imagine how startled we all were? Then we all realized that this was Father's way of saying, "I'm sorry, I was wrong." With this simple act, he restored peace in our family.

That peace was soon shattered by events beyond the family and beyond anything we could imagine. Not long after my father's reconciliation with Duifje, my sister began preparing a new group to leave for Israel. This time, she intended to go with them. But when they were ready to go, it was too late. In May 1940, Hitler invaded Holland.

No one in Holland was prepared for the invasion. Holland was neutral in the war—off limits to either side—and Hitler had assured the Dutch government that he had no intention of breaching that neutrality. The Dutch army did its best to put up resistance, but it was no match for the Germans. Holland capitulated after four days of fighting.

What forced the Dutch capitulation was the relentless German bombing of the city of Rotterdam. At least half of the Dutch casualties were not on the front lines, but among civilians. Nine hundred people were killed, including many schoolchildren. Thousands more were injured, and almost eighty thousand people were left homeless. The devastation was enormous. Hitler threatened to do the same to all the major cities in Holland if the Dutch did not surrender immediately.

A small Dutch Nazi party, led by Anton Mussert and called the NSB (*Nationaal Socialistische Beweging*), had emerged in the years following World War I, but it had never gained much ground with the Dutch people. The NSB turned out to be a so-called fifth column, a group collaborating with the enemy from within by sabotaging the Dutch army. For example, when the invasion started, the Dutch troops carried their ammunition boxes to the front line unaware that the NSB had managed to replace the bullets in some of the boxes with sand. As soon as the Dutch government surrendered, and the Nazis occupied the country, the Germans rewarded their allies by putting NSB members into positions of authority in the police force and in the judicial system. In 1933, Germany descended from being a civilized country into barbarism.

In 1930, the Nazi movement had been considered a joke. In 1943, no one was laughing. The day that fascism marched in through the front door, civilization tiptoed out through the back door. The Nazis themselves were an assault on civilization, and they relied on a very powerful tool to accomplish their ends; they used deception.

The Dutch Jews should have been forewarned. When the Nazis gained power in Germany and began enacting their anti-Semitic policies, German Jews who escaped to Holland told the Dutch Jewish community about the brutality of the Third Reich. But their reports were downplayed by the Dutch Jewish Congress. The congress did not want to alarm the Jewish community, so it told them that the horror stories were exaggerated. Tragically, this *shaa still* ("keep quiet") policy proved fatal for the Dutch Jews. By the time the truth came out, they were no longer able to leave the country.

The shaa still policy of the Dutch Jewish Congress, unfortunately, fed right into the Nazi system of propaganda and censorship. Hitler not only hypnotized people with his speeches, he tightly controlled information that was available in newspapers and on the radio. He controlled what films could appear in movie theatres. He was a master at using the media to misdirect and mislead.

Right up until the Germans marched into Holland, most of the Dutch people, including the Jews, believed that the Nazis would respect the country's neutrality. In the first few months after the occupation, the Germans lulled us into believing that they would not impose their fascist and anti-Semitic policies on the Dutch.

Not everyone was fooled, though! And not all members of the Jewish Congress agreed with the shaa still policy. Soon after the invasion, one member of the congress executive, a dentist who lived a few houses from our family, killed himself, his wife, and their three beautiful daughters by opening the gas valve in their house during the night while everyone was asleep. These girls attended the same school as I did. Learning of their death gave me a terrible shock. Was the dentist right in doing what he did? Knowing what I know now, who am I to judge this act?

Within a few months of the occupation the Germans began to initiate the anti-Jewish laws that would strip away our civil rights. Jews had to wear a Star of David with a large "J" in the centre. We were not allowed to use public transportation or own a car. We were forced to obey a strict curfew. We were not allowed to be on the streets after 8:00 p.m.

As they had in other occupied countries, the Nazis established a Jewish Council, or *Joodse Raad,* to act as intermediaries to the Dutch Jewish community. Most of the members of the Joodse Raad were prominent, middle-class leaders in the Dutch Jewish Congress. They believed that if they co-operated with the Nazi-appointed civilian government they could soften the effects of the Nazis anti-Semitic policies on the Dutch Jewish community. But their hope was in vain. By the fall of 1940 all Jewish newspapers except one had been banned.

Jewish civil servants were forced from their jobs. In the spring and summer of 1941, Jews were barred from public places, schools, and universities. The Germans started seizing Jewish property. Jews had a large "J" stamped in their identity cards.

By the early spring of 1941, we had begun to learn first-hand about Nazi brutality. The Germans were picking up Jews left and right and beating them. In February 1941, a group of Dutch Nazis, now outfitted as police with black uniforms, guns, and high leather boots, decided to have some fun harassing people in the Jewish District. However, they miscalculated;

the Jews did not run away. Some of the young Jewish men had set up defence brigades to protect our community, and they fought back. Non-Jewish men who had been waiting for an opportunity to get their hands on the Dutch Nazis joined in the fight. A riot broke out at the Waterlooplein Square, in Amsterdam, that left one Nazi dead. Dutch Jews were far from passive, as is shown in the historian Jacques Presser's book on the destruction of Dutch Jewry, *Ashes in the Wind.* The records show that Jewish resisters against the Nazis in Holland outnumbered non-Jewish resisters three to one.

The next time they came to harass Jews in the Jewish District, the Dutch Nazis set a trap. They began to taunt the Jews and deliberately incited another riot. Jews and non-Jews came from all sides and fought them, unaware that the German army had closed off all the bridges over the canals and had taken up positions around the area with machine guns so that no one could escape. By the time I arrived with a group of men to join the fight, the steel gates to the bridge over the canal were closed, preventing us from crossing. This part of the city about two blocks from where I lived had now become the Jewish Ghetto.

From then on, all the Jews who lived in Amsterdam were supposed to live in that section. The Germans arrested about four hundred of our men and loaded them onto transport trucks. We found out later that the prisoners had been taken to Mauthausen concentration camp in Austria. None of them survived.

A broader resistance movement started to emerge slowly, but at first it was not very organized. The outlawed Communist Party called a general strike for February 25, 1941. They encouraged all the city employees, especially the streetcar drivers, to cripple the city in retaliation against the Germans. By noon on the 25th, not a single streetcar was running in Amsterdam, and by the end of the day, half of the municipal workers were on strike. The dock workers refused to load and unload the ships in the harbour. They were joined by the metal and shipyard workers, and the strike soon spread to office workers. The next day, the municipal employees went back to work, but other workers joined the strike, so that as many people were out on the streets as had been the day before.

The strike began to spread to other Dutch cities. The Germans had been caught by surprise on the first day of the strike, but by the end of the second day, the commander of the German armed forces declared martial law. Police poured into the streets and rounded up about one hundred men who were thought to be the leaders of the strike. They were arrested and most were deported to concentration camps. The strike had been ruthlessly suppressed.

In April 1942, all Jews over the age of six were forced to wear a yellow Star of David, marked with the word *Jood* (Jew) sewn onto their clothing. A night curfew was imposed for Jews. Jews were forbidden to use public transportation, to have telephones, or even to enter the homes of non-Jews. Soon after, in July 1942, the Nazis began to deport Dutch Jews to the Westerbork concentration camp in Holland, and from there to Auschwitz.

After the suppression of the general strike, resistance to the Nazis went underground. One of the underground actions took place very near my house on March 27, 1943. Around the corner from where I lived was a registration building that contained records of all Dutch citizens, including their religion. The building was closely guarded by the Germans twenty-four hours a day. Every few hours a new group of guards would march in to relieve the guards on duty. On this occasion, however, the relief guards that marched into the building were actually members of the underground dressed in German uniforms. As soon as they got inside the building, they managed to burn all the files in the section where the Jewish records were kept.

Unfortunately, this action did not save the Dutch Jews from their fate. And, for the second time, inaction of the part of the Jewish leaders made them unwilling pawns of the Nazis.

The Joodse Raad kept a record of all the Dutch Jews, carefully listed alphabetically. These records had been compiled by the Dutch Jewish Congress before the war. Council members were urged to destroy the files so that the Germans would not be able to use them to identify the Jews, but they were afraid that by doing so would bring further reprisals against the Jewish community and against themselves. So the files remained intact, and when the time came for the Germans to begin rounding up the Dutch Jews for deportation to the concentration camps, they had neatly kept records to work from. They rounded us up alphabetically.

My oldest sister Esther, whose married name was Buytekant, her husband Jacob, and their son Joseph who was three years older than my daughter Katy lived in the same four-storey house as we did but on a different

The Star of David that we had to sew on all our clothing

floor. Joseph considered himself to be Katy's bodyguard because he was older and very protective of Katy. The Nazis rounded up Esther and her family before the rest of our family. Esther and her family were ordered to step outside their house when their names were called and were then put on a transport truck. We never saw them again.

Esther and Jacob both were deep into the arts, and their apartment was full of valuable paintings. Needless to say we know where all these beautiful paintings and antique pieces ended up! Not even one piece was ever recovered.

The black-uniformed Dutch Nazi police started invading our houses and arresting Jews on the streets. They relentlessly hunted for Jews who tried to escape or were hiding with non-Jews. When Jews were arrested, their

The Hollandse Schouwburg Theatre was back to back with our house

names were entered in a book and their identity cards were confiscated. The Jews were then loaded onto army trucks and taken either to the Hollandse Schouwburg Theatre in Amsterdam, which was being used as a temporary transit station, or they were taken directly to the trains that would transport them to the labour camps. Either way, the Jews were eventually deported to the camps.

When the Nazis first began rounding us up, we did not know anything about concentration camps or extermination camps. We hadn't even heard the words. Between the shaa still policy of the Joodse Raad and the skill and ruthlessness of the Nazi propaganda machine, we had no idea

*The back of our apartment, from which I lowered myself
behind the Hollandse Schouwburg Theatre*

what was in store for us. Nonetheless, I knew enough to seize an opportunity to help some of my Jewish neighbours when I had the chance.

The temporary way station for Amsterdam Jews, the Hollandse Schouwburg Theatre, was in the Plantage Middenlaan, the street right behind where I lived. It is similar to the Royal Alex Theatre in Toronto but larger. The owner was Louise de Vries, a well-known actor. At times, he used to borrow my father's menorah as a stage prop because it was a beautiful large one made of copper with little oil containers and wicks. I knew this theatre and the open space in the back very well because it was

Wedding photo of Henriëtte Les and Michel Engelschmann, August 12, 1942

a playground for me when the theatre was not being used for performances. The theatre's backyard bordered on our backyard, and our fourth-floor veranda was right above it. From this veranda, I could see when people being held in the theatre were occasionally allowed into the open space behind the theatre for some fresh air, and this gave me an idea.

I got some thick rope, made knots in it, fastened it to my veranda, and lowered myself into our backyard. I had already put a stepladder against the fence between our backyard and the open space behind the theatre. By standing on the stepladder, I could talk to the people on the other side of the fence. I asked if any of them wanted help in getting out of there. Several people took me up on my offer. I pulled each one up and over the fence. Once they were safely in our backyard, I moved the stepladder to the other side of the yard, where the fence bordered on a small lane leading out to the street through an alley. I then lowered each person down into the lane, and away they went, through the alley and into the street. They were free—at least for the moment. I helped people escape in this way many times from the beginning of 1942 until I went into hiding, as I describe in the next chapter.

The deportation of Dutch Jews began in June 1942. On August 12, 1942, I married Henrietta Les. Yettie, as she was called, had lived in the Nieuwe

Kerstraat right across from the family Pels since she was born. My oldest sister, Esther, was related to the Pelses by marriage. Yettie and I became close friends with the Pels family. We knew their children, Katy and Philip, from the time they were born.

Yettie worked in a factory that made German uniforms, and because of her work she was given a pass, an official note stating that she worked for the Germans. If she was ever picked up for deportation, all she had to do was show the paper to the authorities and they would let her go. This was supposed to apply to me too, but it didn't work out that way. We soon learned that the German authorities could not be trusted to honour Yettie's "spare." Ignorant as we all were about the "forced labour camps," Yettie and I thought that because we were married, when our turn came to be deported we would be able to stay together. How wrong we were.

CHAPTER TWO

Deportation

WHEN MY OLDEST SISTER, ESTHER, AND HER FAMILY WERE DEPORTED, MUCH of our grief came from our feelings of helplessness. There was nothing we could do to prevent it. The lowest class of human beings, the Nazis, were now the masters, and they ruled with terror, including guns. Anyone who spoke out against them was shot on the spot or deported to face a slower death. But we still did not understand how hopeless things really were.

During the war, cash had very little value and, to protect what wealth they had, people in general bought all the diamonds, silverware, figurines, and gold pieces that they could get their hands on. When they realized that they might soon be deported, many of my father's Jewish clients asked him, as their accountant, to be the guardian of their valuables. They believed that because of his age—he was then fifty-eight years old—and because he had a heart problem, he would not be deported to a forced labour camp.

So each client made a small package containing their valuables and delivered it to our home. All of our relatives, including our immediate family, did the same with their jewellery. Instead of using the client's name, my father numbered each package so that, when everything returned to normal, the valuables could be identified. Then we set about hiding the packages. My father's office was in our house, in a room with a built-in closet where he stored all his bookkeeping files and account books. My father and I cut out a space inside the wall directly above the closet and stuffed all the packages into the space. We then closed up the wall and repapered the whole room so that there was no evidence of our hiding place. For everyone's protection, none of my father's clients knew the identity of any other client who had given us valuables for safekeeping. It was a good idea, but, unfortunately, in case neither he nor I survived the war, my father told each client separately where the packages were hidden. I would discover later that this was a mistake.

After we had already closed up the wall and restored the room to its normal condition, another of my father's clients arrived with two leather briefcases full of gold coins and asked my father to take care of them. We didn't want to risk breaking the wall open again, so my father decided to ask someone else to keep the contents of the two briefcases safe.

The person my father had chosen to guard the gold was a non-Jewish man who had taken over a business belonging to one of my father's Jewish clients for the duration of the war. A number of Jews tried to protect their businesses from the Nazis in this way. The Jews hoped that by naming a non-Jew as the legal owner of the business, they would stop the Nazis from taking it over and putting their own *verwalter,* or manager, in charge. We could not transport the briefcases during the day. We had to do it during the night when Jews were not allowed to be on the street. It was a dangerous mission.

We put pieces of rope around the briefcases to reinforce them because they were heavy and, because Jews were no longer allowed to use public transportation, we had to walk quite a distance with them. My father and I delivered the briefcases to a house somewhere in the neighbourhood of the Lineus Straat, and then we walked back to our house. This was all done in total darkness because the city was blacked out against air raid attacks. During the walk back, my father told me that, in addition to our hidden package of valuables, he had also given some of our money to our non-Jewish neighbour across the street, Mr. Biermasz, for safekeeping. If any of us survived the war and needed money, we would be able to go to Mr. Biermasz and get it. Mr. Biermasz was in charge of the laboratory in the building across the street from us and lived on the top floor. His windows were right across from ours. He saw me several times as I escaped over the tiled, peaked roof, so I was forced to walk through the gutters.

It was in April 1942 that we were forced to wear a large yellow Star of David to make it easier for the Nazis to round up and arrest the Jews. My sister Duifje married Herman Duizend in early April of 1942. There was no wedding party.

My family was rounded up in August 1942, not long after Yettie and I were married. More than fifty years have passed, and it is still very difficult for me to write about this. Our turn to be deported had come. We were packed into the back of a German army truck and transported to a building in the Euterpe Straat for booking. Our ID cards (with the large "J" for Jew) were taken away from us. When it was my turn to hand over my ID card, I showed the authorities the letter stating that my wife was working in a factory that manufactured German uniforms. Without a word, I was unceremoniously taken to a side door and practically thrown out of the building. I never had a chance to say goodbye to my family.

Jews who were rounded up were told that they were being resettled for work in Eastern Europe, and that they should take some of their personal belongings with them. That was the lie that was used to deceive the Jews. That was how so many Jews were transported to the gas chambers with so little resistance. We didn't have the slightest idea what was actually going on.

When my family was picked up by the Nazis, called out alphabetically as my older sister had been, we were given no time to collect our belongings. We were simply ordered out of our house, into the street, and onto a transport truck. Because we had all been told to bring our personal belongings, when I was released I went home and packed some things for my parents and my sisters. I even specially packed boxes filled with cigars for my father. We now know what happened to these articles that Jews were told to bring with them: everything was shipped to Germany and given to the Germans. Nothing ever reached the prisoners in the concentration camps. My father never got his cigars. The German people were only too happy to make good use of all the things they took from the Jews.

I did one more thing when I returned to my house after being released. I hid all our family photographs, passports, and identity cards inside a wall in the house. I cut a slot in the wall and slid the documents and photographs down behind the wallpaper.

The next day, as I stood alone on our fourth-floor balcony, I saw a black-uniformed policeman walking below. I was so filled with sadness and anger about my family being taken from me that I began to taunt him, shouting, "Hey big boy, come on upstairs without your gun so we can have a heart-to-heart talk. Just the two of us." I know that it was a stupid thing to do, but all I can say is that I was not in my right mind at that moment. The policeman didn't look up or say anything.

A few weeks after this incident, however, the Gestapo paid me a visit. They wanted to know where the jewellery and valuables were hidden. I was stunned and told them that I didn't know anything about this. They knocked me around a bit and told me they did not really need my assistance because they knew exactly where to find the jewellery. Just then, one of the Gestapo men, accompanied by another man, came upstairs. He was carrying an axe. He went straight to the wall above the built-in closet, cut it open, removed all the packages, and tore them open. What came out of there was unbelievable. There were loose diamonds, gold cigarette cases with ruby snap locks, gold watches, small gold figurines, diamond rings, and diamond and gold necklaces and bracelets, including articles that belonged to my own family.

The Gestapo men began to hurl questions at me. What was the meaning of the numbers on each package? Who were the owners? I told them that I didn't have the faintest idea, that my father had never talked to us about his clients. What I didn't know then was that one of my father's clients had been arrested, and that he was the man who had come upstairs with the member of the Gestapo. He had been sitting in the Gestapo car in front of our house until he was brought into our home to show the Gestapo where the jewellery was hidden. The Gestapo hoped that he could tell them who the valuables belonged to, so they could identify and find Jews who were in hiding. But he couldn't tell them. At the time, I assumed that he had been trying to buy his freedom by promising to give some jewellery to the Gestapo. In fact, they had already beaten this man so badly that he had broken down and told the Gestapo where his own jewellery was hidden. But he had had no idea that other valuables were hidden there as well.

The Gestapo then started to get rough with me. They put me against the wall underneath our grandfather clock, held a gun to my head, and said, "You have three minutes to remember the names of the other people." I didn't particularly like having a gun held to my head, but, after about two minutes, I said to them, "Two minutes are up, so I guess that I have one minute more to live. I don't know whose jewellery this is. My father never talked to us about his clients, and, even if you shoot me now, I still would not be able to tell you their names."

Amazingly enough this seemed to make sense to the Gestapo. They picked up the jewellery, put it back in the boxes, took the boxes downstairs to their car, and drove off. For a short time I felt relieved. The idiots were so busy roughing me up that they had completely overlooked the shelves with my father's bookkeeping records. All the names they were looking for were right under their noses! I realized that I had to find a way to get rid of those books. I could not take a chance that the people named in them had not yet been rounded up or that they were in hiding.

I decided that the best way to dispose of the books was to burn them; easier said than done. First I had to rip them up and then put them in a little hearth in the front room. It was a closed hearth, fed by coal, and burning those heavy books was going to take a very long time. I was only able to work on this during the day because at night, Amsterdam was under a complete blackout, and the smoke and fire could be seen. Anyone who used lights inside the house at night had to have their windows covered with black paper. The Germans made very sure that no one broke the rules.

One night, Yettie was helping me tear up the books to prepare them for burning the next day. We ripped apart all the records and ledgers that my father had in his office: between seventy-five and a hundred ledger books, all made of heavy paper. As we were working, I happened to glance out the uncovered front windows and noticed a car turning into our street. Something made me say to Yettie, "Hurry downstairs to the neighbours and don't come back up, no matter what you hear. Just remember that as long as you are free, I will find a way to escape." I had a gut feeling that I was about to get another unannounced visitor. My intuition turned out to be correct. One of the Gestapo officers came up the stairs carrying a flashlight. There was no time to hide anything, so I met him at the top of the stairway, blocking his view of the front room. He asked me what I was doing there in the dark. I couldn't afford to let him see the mess that Yettie and I had made, so as he shone his flashlight around, I told him that I could not put on the light because there was no blackout paper on the windows. I asked him not to play around with his flashlight so much because the guards outside would shoot at any window that had lights shining through them. To my surprise, he actually switched it off and announced that he had come to pick me up for questioning at headquarters.

That didn't sound very promising, but my greater concern right then was keeping him away from the front room. The bathroom door was close to the top of the stairs, so I told him that I had to go to the bathroom very badly. He said that I could, but he checked the bathroom first, to make sure that there was no way for me to escape. While I was in the bathroom, he stood in front of the door, and when I was finished, I went downstairs with him. There was a car waiting with a driver and the two of them took me to a jail. I think it was on the Amstelveense Weg.

Several times over the next few days I was taken by car from the jail to Gestapo headquarters for interrogation. They kept asking me how much jewellery the men from the Gestapo had taken from my house. I got the impression that some of the jewellery had disappeared between my house and Gestapo headquarters. I told them some of what I had seen, but I was careful not to give them too full a description of the valuables that had been uncovered. I was afraid that if some of the Gestapo men had pocketed some of the jewellery and if I gave evidence to their superiors, I might end up getting "accidentally" shot by one of them during my travels to and from their headquarters.

Each day, after about an hour of interrogation, I was taken back to the jail. On one of the trips, I noticed that the officers had forgotten to lock the back door of the car. When a streetcar came toward us, I seized the opportunity to escape. I jumped out of the car, ran in the opposite direction behind the streetcar, and hopped onto the open platform. Then I moved to the front of the streetcar, jumped off as soon as I saw another streetcar coming the other way, and boarded it. By then, the Gestapo had turned their car around and were following the first streetcar, not knowing that I was already travelling on another streetcar in the opposite direction.

I knew that I could not go back to my house, so I went to the funeral home where my Jewish neighbour who lived in the apartment right below mine worked as a carpenter, making caskets in the upstairs workshop. I asked for the key so I could stay there. I knew that the funeral home was a very safe place to go because their superstition would have kept the Germans from going in. They would have put a guard in front to watch any comings and goings, but they would never have entered the building. The funeral home is still there, but the front entrance has been changed.

After getting the key, I went up to the roof of our building. We had very steep roofs in Amsterdam, but the gutters were wide and strong. My best friend, Ado Broodboom, lived right around the corner from me, and we made a point of leaving our attic windows unlocked so that we could walk along the eavestroughs to each other's houses. I went around the corner to the side street where Ado lived. His window was open, so I climbed inside, went downstairs to the street, walked to the funeral home in the Nieuwe Kerstraat, and let myself in. For the next three weeks, I slept in a casket. Ado checked my house regularly and, after about three weeks, he told me that it was safe to go back. The Gestapo were no longer watching the house.

As I mentioned earlier, Ado was black. His father had come to Holland from Surinam, in South America, in 1920, and his mother was Dutch. Ado was born in Amsterdam in 1922 and was only two years old when his father died. Ado and I have been close friends since we were very young. The fact that his skin was a different colour from mine had not meant a thing to me until I heard someone making a remark. Children don't notice things like that. No one is born a racist. We are taught to be racists. As my friend, Ado was always welcome in our home. When my father made kiddush or havdalah (the blessing over the wine at the beginning and end of the Sabbath), there was always some wine for Ado.

Ado and I had become friends when we were boys, hanging around with the other kids from our neighbourhood who were mostly Jewish. Somehow Ado and I formed a closer bond. I was very interested when Ado started his musical career by learning to play the accordion. Our families also decided that we should learn how to dance because it would teach us to be more graceful. But we both had two left feet when it came to dancing. Ado the coward figured out a way to skip the classes. He made a deal with the owner of the dance studio. As long as Ado did not have to join in, he would provide music for the classes by playing his accordion.

Ado also learned to play the trumpet and studied at the Conservatory in Amsterdam. One of his teachers was Marinus Komst, first trumpeter of the Concertgebouw Orchestra in Amsterdam. Marinus passed away in 2003. Ado is a wonderful musician. The United States may have had Louis Armstrong, but in Holland, we had Ado Broodboom. He later became a member of the Ramblers, one of the best bands in Holland.

During the war, although Ado was black he was not in as much danger as the Jews. According to the Nazis, his turn would come after they had dealt with the Jews. In the meantime, he found ways to play his music. Ado could play two trumpets at the same time in harmony, and one of his famous numbers was "Tiger Rag." The German troops loved listening to it, but by then the band had renamed the song "Der Schwarze Panther." By listening to forbidden English radio, the band picked up new songs and gave them German names so that they would not get censored.

Soon after I moved back into my house, I bought a short-wave radio that was about the size of a portable television set so that Ado and I could listen to the British newscasts and find out what was happening in the war. I installed the radio in my room in the attic. To make a flat antenna, I crawled up to the peak of the roof, installed insulators, and put a wire across and down into my room. I did all this right under the noses of the Germans who were guarding the Jews in the theatre behind my house.

A few weeks later, I was again honoured by a visit from the Gestapo. As Ado and I were listening to the English news broadcast, we heard someone at the door downstairs. I said to Ado, "Get out of here fast. Use the roof while I go downstairs." Sure enough, the same officer came up the stairs. He looked around and said, "You have an extra room here, haven't you?" Being Jewish, I answered his question with a question: "And where would that be?" "All the houses in this district have attics," he replied, "I want to see your attic." The last thing I wanted was for this man to see my room in the attic, so I told him that all that was up there was some coal for the furnace. He walked up the stairs with me and said, pointing to the door to my bedroom, "I want this door open." I told him that the room belonged to the neighbours below me. He gave me a choice: either I opened the door or he would do it for me with his foot. Stalling for time, I pretended to go to the neighbour to ask for the key, which was actually in my pocket because I knew as soon as the door opened, the first thing he would see was the radio tuned to the English station. Jews were not supposed to have radios, and they were certainly not supposed to have radios tuned to the English newscast. I had no choice but to open the door, thinking that this was the end of me. But when we entered the room, the radio was gone. I was flabbergasted! The Gestapo official looked around and said, "There's nothing in this room." I asked him what he was looking for, but he walked out of the house without answering.

When he had gone, I went over the roof to Ado's place and asked him what had happened. Where was the radio? He said, "I didn't think it a good idea to leave the radio there, so I took it with me over the roof and as soon as I found another house with an open window, I dropped it off in an empty room."

We soon went back to pick up the radio, but I didn't install it again because I knew that the Gestapo were keeping their eye on me. I decided not to stay in my place anymore and moved some of my belongings over to my wife's parents' house, where Yettie was living. So far, her family had managed to avoid being rounded up. They had a hidden stairwell in their house that led to a small cellar underneath the house. The entrance to this stairwell was built so that you had to lift up part of the floor inside a walk-in closet to get into it. Yettie's parents had nailed a small rug on top of the part that had to be lifted up, so that when the trapdoor was closed, no one could tell that there was an entrance beneath it. The cellar was used as a hiding-place whenever there was either a roundup or a *razzia* (police raid). A roundup was a methodical, alphabetical, gathering up of all the Jews in a given area; a razzia, on the other hand, was a random sweep in which Jews were literally taken off the streets or dragged out of their houses. In the end, however, it made little difference to the Jews who were transported to the camps whether the Nazis had picked them up methodically or at random.

Early one morning, after my wife had left the house, I was still in bed when I heard the sound of someone breaking down the front door. I ran to the shelter where my in-laws were already hiding. I tried to open the trap-door but saw that I was too late. I got away from the closet just as the Nazis came into the house on the main floor. They asked me where the family was. "I don't know," I said, "because I was sound asleep when you woke me up by breaking down the door." The Nazis gave me a severe beating, and then arrested me and transported me with other Jews to the Hollandse Schouwburg Theatre. It so happened, though, that there was one guard in the back of the truck with the prisoners. I knew exactly the route that this truck was taking, so I was prepared when we came to a curve in the road that was so sharp the guard would have to hang on with both hands. I only had to hit him once to make him go down. I jumped off over the tail-gate right in front of my house and opened the front door. I ran upstairs to the roof and over to Ado's place. From that moment on, I knew that I could no longer stay in either my house or my wife's parents' house. I had to disappear.

I removed the Star of David from my clothing and stayed with Ado for a few days. By this time, Ado was playing trumpet and accordion in a band. The band had an English name, Micro Rhythm Club, but the German authorities ordered them to change it so the band then became known as "Louis Van Der Steen and His Soloists." When the band got some engagements outside of Amsterdam, I travelled with them as their "band boy," that is, I helped move equipment and set up for their performances. After about a month we ended up in the city of Breda, where the band was booked to play at the Lindeboom Dance Hall for a longer contract. Since I was going to be there for a while, I rented a room and asked Yettie to join me. She agreed, and so I went to meet her in Amsterdam and the two of us travelled by train to Breda.

In the railway station at Breda Yettie and I were stopped by a member of the NSB police who asked me in German if I was a Jew. I said yes. He asked me again, I said yes again. Then he asked me the same question in Dutch, and I said, "No, where did you get that idea?" He replied, "But you answered yes before." I told him that I did not know what he was talking about because I could not speak German. I was not just trying to play games with him. I had tried to confuse him with my answers because I could tell that he was Dutch and I wanted to divert his attention away from Yettie. I was afraid that he would try to question her and she did not have false identification papers, while I had gotten a false identity card through Ado. My ruse was successful. He checked only my identity card, and he told us both to go.

I had installed an alarm system wired through the basements of a number of houses in the same block as my wife's family's house. Anyone living in the houses who spotted a roundup or a razzia could push a button to activate a bell inside all the wired houses as a warning for everyone to get into their hiding places. Our good friends Rika and Max Pels lived across the street from Yettie's family home. Whenever the warning bell rang, Rika and Max Pels would put their children, Katy and Philip, into the basement between two piles of coal, and warn them not to cry. The priority for the Dutch Nazi police, during a rounding up of Jews, was to get at the children first. That way the parents would automatically come out of their hiding places and surrender. Katy, who was three and a half, comforted one-year-old Philip so that he would be quiet. After the razzia was over, Rika would go downstairs and pick up the two children, who were covered in black coal dust.

On several occasions Max and Rika had discussed the possibility of sending Katy and Philip into hiding outside Amsterdam. After going through the nerve-wracking ordeal of the razzia one too many times, all of Rika's maternal instincts told her that her children's survival was at stake. This time the decision was made to send the children away for their own safety.

All the Nazi-occupied countries in Europe had special sections of underground resistance groups that were dedicated to saving Jewish children. The networks, usually organized by Jews and Christians working together, operated mostly through personal contacts. For their own protection, Jewish children were taken from their homes, separated from their family and friends, and either given refuge in convents and orphanages or adopted and protected by courageous non-Jewish families. Some "hidden" Jewish children were able to disguise their Jewishness with Christian names and made-up identities, and some had to literally disappear from sight, hiding in attics, basements, haylofts, barns, or closets. They all had to learn at a very early age to lie about who they really were, to hide their emotions, and to remain silent, watchful, and alert in dangerous situations.

Very occasionally, whole families were able to hide together, or one parent or another family member was able to hide with the child, but most of the time young children were sent far away, frightened and alone, and entrusted to complete strangers. Often, the people who offered shelter knew that the children were Jewish, but sometimes not even the foster parents knew that the children they were sheltering were Jews.

When Max and Rika made their difficult decision to send Katy and Philip into hiding, they got word out to the underground. The children were soon picked up and taken to a rural area in the southern part of Holland, in the province of Limburg. Their cover story was that the children were orphans whose parents had been killed during the bombardment of Rotterdam. For everyone's safety, Rika and Max were never told where the children were being hidden. And now that Katy and Philip were being taken care of, their parents felt free to go into hiding themselves. Hiding a whole family together would have been too difficult and too dangerous.

While Yettie and I were living in the rented room in Breda, Rika Pels showed up and told us that she needed a place to stay until she could find another hiding place. She had changed her appearance to match her false identity card. She had dyed curly blond hair and looked just like a "lady of the evening." She was on her own; her husband, Max, had stayed behind in hiding in Amsterdam, and their children, Katy and Philip, were being hidden somewhere in the Dutch countryside.

Of course, Yettie and I let her stay with us in Breda. Max Pels and I had made a pact to look after each other's family. I promised him that if he and Rika did not return after the war, I would try to find the children, bring them back to Amsterdam, and look after them. He promised me that if I didn't return, he would look after Yettie.

One day, while I was trying to improve something on my false identity card, I made a mess out of it. Ado had to go back to Amsterdam for a few days, so I asked him to look for another card. When he returned, I thought that maybe he had been unable to get another card, so I looked at him and said, "Noooo?" But he answered, "Yes!" So I knew that he must have hidden the card somewhere on him. I took a guess. "Take it out of your shoe," I said. And that's exactly where it was. It goes to show you how well we knew each other. In our neighbourhood people used to call us brothers.

Now that I had another identity card, I had to make it my own by removing the owner's picture and putting on my own. With India ink and a special pen, I drew the part of the stamp on my own picture that matched the stamp already on the card. It was very precise work and needed a lot of patience. While I was in the middle of working on the card in my room, the landlady walked in without any warning. I had no chance to cover up what I was doing, and I could tell that she had seen it. She didn't say a word, but as soon as she left the room, I packed some of our belongings and the three of us, Rika, Yettie, and I, moved to a room in another house.

While all of this was going on, Ado was back in Amsterdam. He had gone for the weekend and I had asked him to take my watch in to be repaired. When he returned, I told him what happened. He said he would keep an eye on the place because one could never be sure who would try to make some extra money by selling us out to the Nazis. After a few days, everything looked safe and we decided to return to our original room. That proved to be a big mistake. No sooner were we back in our room when three men from the NSB police walked in and without a word arrested the three of us. They took us to their headquarters in the castle, the Burght. This was in May 1943, less than a year after my family was taken away.

CHAPTER THREE

From the Burght to Vught—
and Auschwitz

IN THE BURGHT, THE NSB POLICE QUESTIONED YETTIE, RIKA, AND ME— the kind of questioning that left me bleeding and bruised all over. In no way was I going to tell them how and where I had gotten my fake ID card. I insisted that it was mine. They decided to send Yettie and me to a concentration camp. Because I had been seen making a false identity card, the Nazis concluded that I must have been connected to the underground. But Rika's false identity card was in the name of a lady of the night (*Hoer*) in Amsterdam, and when the police checked out her card by phone, they found that the descriptions matched. Both women had blond curly hair and, as I mentioned earlier, Rika had made herself look the part. So Rika was escorted to the train station and put on the train to Amsterdam, with the words, "We don't need your kind in Breda. In Amsterdam you could do much more business."

Yettie and I were put on an army truck with guards and taken to the concentration camp in Vught, Holland, to be dehumanized. We had no idea where we were.

The fences that divided the women's and men's barracks were electrically charged on both sides. Touching them would be instant death. The women's and men's barracks were divided by a fence with a walkway in between for the guards. Yettie was put in a women's barracks located on one side of the fence, and I was put in a barracks on the other side with non-Jewish prisoners. The Vught camp in Holland should have been a warning of things to come. Jewish and non-Jewish prisoners were kept completely separate, and because of my false identity card, the camp authorities did not realize that I was Jewish, and I was in no hurry to tell them otherwise. Non-Jewish prisoners were more likely to have been arrested for political or criminal reasons and, in general, they were treated less harshly than the Jewish prisoners. Since the police who had sent me to Vught believed that I was part of the underground, they put me in the non-Jewish section of the camp. In those barracks, I was entitled to receive a parcel from the Red Cross that contained cookies, sugar, and cigarettes. The parcels were handed out about once a month to non-Jewish prisoners only.

As far as Jewish concentration camp prisoners were concerned, the Red Cross might as well have been under Hitler's command. The Jews never received any parcels from the Red Cross.

By this time, the Allied forces had taken a number of German prisoners, who were being held in special prisoner-of-war camps in England, Canada, and the United States. By using the German prisoners as leverage, the International Red Cross could have declared the Jews to be prisoners of war. If Hitler had been forced to accept this declaration, the Nazis would have had to treat the Jews in the concentration camps as prisoners of war, according to international law. Instead, once we were inside the concentration camps, the Nazis treated us as lower than animals. Even a dog has a name. Jews had only numbers. We were in a constant state of hunger and terror. We never knew what would happen next.

When I got my first Red Cross parcel in Vught, I decided to throw it over the fence to the women's side, in the hope that I could get it to my wife. I saw a woman walking on the other side and asked her to give the parcel to Yettie. She promised to do so, but just as I threw the parcel over the fence, a guard spotted me. He took me to the guardhouse and told the other guards what I had done. They all decided that I should be punished. While they were deciding what form that punishment should take, another prisoner, who was also the camp carpenter, walked in with a new contraption that he had been ordered to build. Any prisoner who had skills that were useful to the Nazis was forced to use those skills to provide various services to the camp authorities. In this case, the camp carpenter, who also was a prisoner, had been ordered to construct an instrument of torture known as *der bock* (rack), a curved four-legged frame with leather straps on each leg to secure the prisoner's ankles and wrists.

The guards decided to try out their new device. They put me on the contraption, face down, and strapped my arms and legs to the legs of the bock. Then the five guards took turns whipping me with a large leather whip with knots in it. They each hit me five times. They forced me to count the strokes and warned me not to make any mistakes. If I said "eleven" and the count was ten, they would start all over again until I had properly counted my twenty-five lashes. When they were finished, my striped prison uniform was ripped to shreds and so was the skin on my back. I was thrown out of the guardhouse and told to go back to my barracks. As I limped across the square, I heard somebody calling my name. It was a cousin of mine who was in one of the Jewish barracks. I hadn't known that he was in the camp. He called across the square, "Hi, Mike, how are you?" I called back that I was all right, although while I was standing there, my shoes were filling up with blood from the whipping I had received.

By the time I got back to my barracks, the block *elderster* (a prisoner, usually German, who was in charge of the barracks) had already heard what had happened. He said that I had made history by being the first prisoner to get twenty-five lashes on the brand-new bock. I told him that I could not refuse this honour. He put some Vaseline on my back and found me a fresh uniform. The welts on my back eventually healed, but some of the scars are still there.

All the guards in the Vught concentration camp were Dutch. These Dutch guards were as bad and in some cases worse than the German guards. The camp guards took great delight in tormenting the prisoners. For example, one day they called out the men in our barracks and ordered us to go outside the camp. To do that, we had to walk between two rows of guards. Each guard had a specially trained German shepherd on a leash. When the guard said the word "Jew," the dog would go into a frenzy. As we walked between the guards, we were told to pick up leaves from the ground with our hands and put them on a pile, and so quite a few of us got nipped by the dogs. While we were picking up the leaves and the guards were teasing their dogs, one of the guards took off his cap and threw it behind him into the trees. He then pointed to one of the prisoners and ordered him to get his cap back.

Fortunately, before we were marched out of the campground, a prisoner from another barracks had warned us all never to turn our backs to any guard while we were going through their line. So the prisoner who had been ordered to retrieve the guard's cap knew enough to walk backwards through the line of guards, pick up the cap, walk forward back to the guard, and return his cap, never once turning his back to the guard. If he had turned his back to the guard, the guard would have shot him, claiming that the prisoner had tried to escape. And as a reward for shooting the prisoner, the guard would have been given three days off duty and extra cigarette rations. In the games that the guards played with us at Vught, there was no referee.

It was in the early spring of 1943 that I was put on a train and transported along with other, mostly Jewish, prisoners to Poland. Other prisoners who stayed behind in Vught told us that prisoners who were transported out of the camp were never told where they were going and, wherever it was, there would certainly be no welcoming committee when they arrived. That is where they were wrong. It turns out that there was a welcoming committee, a selection committee whose members decided the fate of the newly arrived prisoners. They decided who would live at least a little longer, and who would die immediately.

The train that took us to Poland was a cattle train with no seats. We had to either stand up or lay halfway down on the straw that was on the floor. There was a barrel that we used as a toilet. I didn't know whether Yettie was on the train. On the transport, they realized I was a Jew and marked me accordingly. I do not remember how long it took us to get to Auschwitz, the most notorious of all the Nazi concentration camps. But when we arrived, the "welcoming committee" made their selections. Not that we knew what any of this was about. All we knew was that some of us were told to stand in one line, and others were told to join another line. Those who went in the other line were never seen again.

Because I arrived in Auschwitz on a Jewish transport train from Vught, and received the same prison uniform as all the others, that is, a uniform marked with a Jewish identity tag, from that moment on I was identified as a Jew. Our group was marched off to one of the barracks. It was not long afterward that we had to march to the concentration camp Birkenau. We had to stand in a line-up to be tattooed. It was there that my name was changed into number 163256, which was tattooed onto my left arm, and while we were being tattooed we witnessed a brutal incident that is still very hard to talk about.

The *kapo,* or head, of the work detail that was tattooing the new arrivals was a German prisoner. One of the men in our group called out to him, saying, "Hey, Hans, I know you. We went to school together." Without a further word, two of the kapo's helpers picked up this prisoner and put him in front of the kapo. They laid him down on the floor, face up, and a third helper brought over a shovel, and with full force, pushed the shovel through the man's neck and decapitated him. We watched in total disbelief. There was nothing we could do because we were surrounded by soldiers with their guns trained on us. The guards certainly didn't care. They enjoyed watching one prisoner killing another. We were sick to our stomachs. After the body of the poor man was thrown out of the barracks, the kapo called out, "Is there anyone else here who thinks they know me?" No one said a word …

That is how I was introduced to the behaviour of the people who controlled the Nazi concentration camps. I will not call them beasts. It would be an insult to animals. The people in charge of us were all murderers and crooks. They were the *Reichs-Deutchers,* German-born criminals who were put into the concentration camps to be our masters. After this incident we were marched off to another barracks. There we were handed our uniforms and a small identity tag with our number on it, to be sewn onto our jackets. My tag, a Star of David, identified me as a Jew. Some of the other prisoners in the camp had tags that identified them, for example, as political prisoners (red triangle), Jehovah's Witnesses (purple triangle), and homosexuals (pink triangle with an "A" inside it).

Our uniform was a striped jacket and pair of pants. Our heads were shaved, so everyone was bald when they came out of the barracks. We were then taken to our barracks, where the block elderster in charge assigned me a bunk bed that was covered with a little straw. After we had all been assigned beds, he made very sure that we knew the rules and regulations that we would have to follow in the camp. Not following even the smallest rule could mean instant death. If any of us had managed to arrive with any illusions about what the Nazis had in store for us, they were now shattered.

CHAPTER FOUR

The Coal Mines of Janina
and the Buna Works

A COUPLE OF DAYS AFTER MY ARRIVAL IN BIRKENAU, I WAS MOVED AGAIN, to another section of the vast complex. This time I was taken by transport truck to the Janina camp to work in the coal mine. The work was very hard and we got very little food. Most prisoners did not last more than three months there. Civilians were also working in this coal mine; as far as I know they were Polish people. They were not allowed to talk to us, but I noticed that when they had their break, they had something to eat as they were sitting on the floor of the shaft. When they got up to start working again, we found that some of them had left their scraps for us. They made sure that the guards could not see this because they would have been severely punished.

I worked the night shift, and every morning when we marched out of the mine, guards were waiting to take us back to the camp. Just like the guards at Vught, these guards had their own way of having some fun at our expense.

Every morning, after a long night's work, they would order us to lie down on the ground, to do push-ups, roll over, and march in place in the mud. Can you picture what we looked like? Only after we did what the guards ordered us to do were we allowed to pick up our ration of bread and go to our barracks to sleep. And after we had been allowed to rest for a short time, the guards would call us out for roll call. If it suited them, they would order us to start the exercises all over again. We got very little sleep. The camp commander did not care that the prisoners didn't last very long. He could get fresh recruits whenever he needed them. Life was cheap. As far as the Nazis were concerned, all they had to do was to give the prisoners a few scraps of bread, work them hard, and when they died, replace them with new ones.

To add insult to injury, when Christmas came, the guards made us sing "Holy Night" for them before we went down into the mine.

One morning in January 1944, we marched out of the mine shaft and then were told to stop. One of the guards ordered all electricians to step out of the line. I didn't move because I had never told them that I was an electrician. But somebody else must have told them, because the next thing I knew, the butt of a rifle hit my neck, forcing me to step out of the line. As far as I can remember, one other person stepped forward. We were both taken by truck to the concentration camp in Buna.

In my new barracks, the block elderster, who is usually a German prisoner, assigned me to a top bunk. When I climbed up to it I found another fellow in my bed. To my delight, not only was he Dutch, he was also from Amsterdam. His name was Joseph De Jong, and everyone in the barracks called him Joe. He decided our meeting was cause for a celebration, and he pulled a cigarette butt out of his pocket and offered it to me. I told him that I did not smoke, so he lit the butt. As soon as he started to smoke, the block elderster shouted, "Who is smoking here? Step forward immediately." I took one look at Joe and saw the shape he was in. He was skin and bones, about 110 pounds (50 kilogams). I could see that he would not be able to take much punishment, so I climbed down and faced the block elderster. I explained that, because I had just arrived, I did not know the rules very well. He hit me a few times with the rubber hose and warned me that the next time I would not get off so lightly. This little incident created a bond between Joe and me. We decided that from that moment on, we would share whatever we could "organize," that is, whatever we could steal from the Germans.

The concentration camp in Buna supplied slave labour for IG Farben Industries, a huge conglomerate of chemical manufacturers. In fact, the new Buna-Monowitz section of Auschwitz was built expressly to house the prisoners working at IG Farben's new factory. The Buna works, within walking distance of the camp, would be producing synthetic fuel and synthetic rubber for Hitler's secret weapons, the v-1 and v-2 rockets.

According to our guards, the v-1 and v-2 rockets were the secret weapons that Hitler was going to use to win the war. And I was given the dubious honour of working on them.

The morning after I arrived at Buna, I was taken to the factory where I met the civilian electrical engineer who was in charge of this installation, Obermeister ("overseer") Ritter. He showed me some blueprints and asked if I could wire a section of the factory. I told him that I could, as long as I had the right tools and some people to help me.

In camp the following day, my number was called out of the roll call. I stepped out in front of the line and the camp commander asked for electrician's helpers. Several other prisoners came forward and said that they were electricians. I called Joe to stand with me, saying that he was also an expert electrician. We now had thirty-five prisoners, all of them supposedly electricians, none of whom had probably ever used a screwdriver and all of whom were likely terrified of electricity. But they all had one thing in common. They were trying to escape from the back-breaking manual labour they were doing inside the camp, digging large pits, loading mine carts with sand and gravel and then pushing them on tracks, running with heavily laden wheelbarrows to please the guards. We were marched off to the part of the factory that had to be wired, the section where they would be manufacturing the synthetic rubber.

Mr. Ritter walked in with six English prisoners of war and told me to use them for any kind of work that was necessary. He also handed me requisition forms for tools, an electrical tester, materials to start the job, and a small dolly with four wheels to be used for picking up tools, equipment, and materials. Incidentally, that same electrical tester now hangs in a showcase in the Holocaust Educational Centre in the Lipa Green Building in Toronto.

I put Joe in charge of the dolly so that he would not have to prove his skill as an electrician. Joe was a furrier by trade, and this way he would not have to do any of the heavy work, such as cutting holes in concrete walls with a hammer and chisel. There were no electrical drills then. Once I had shown him where to pick up materials, he had the freedom to roam around on the property as long as he had a signed requisition form from me.

There were guards all around the property as well as inside the factory. My job was to wire up the machines and install the motors. I was instructed not to have any conversation with the English soldiers, except to show them what I needed them to do. My English was about as good as my Chinese, and I do not speak any Chinese! However, it is amazing how much conversation you can have if both sides are willing to understand each other.

Every morning when we arrived at the factory with our crew, the kapo in charge handed me a requisition for the forty litres of soup that our *commando,* or work crew, would be allowed for lunch. The camp's kitchen staff delivered the soup in a kind of thermos drum kettle that was left at the side of the road at noon. Joe and a helper had to pick up the soup kettle with his dolly. The English soldiers got their own ration of soup, which Joe picked up at the same time.

Our crew usually arrived at the plant at about 7:00 a.m. One morning, as we arrived for work, I saw that one of the English soldiers, named Burt, had brought along two sets of boxing gloves. Burt asked another soldier if he wanted to go a few rounds with him before work started, but he said no. The other soldiers all declined as well. I saw an opportunity to do some business and asked Burt if he wanted to spar with me for a few rounds. I told him that I used to box, although not in his class because he weighed about 180 pounds (82 kilograms) and I weighed about 115 pounds (52 kilograms). So we agreed that we would just have a workout and that there would be no damaging punches. We also agreed that, in exchange for the workout, I would get their requisition for the lunch soup. The English prisoners of war did not have to rely on the soup that we all got at lunch. They were given much better food to eat in addition to their Red Cross packages, so they did not mind giving up their soup ration. Their requisition was for ten litres, which I promptly changed to twenty litres so that our whole crew could get extra soup.

The soup was made of hot water and cauliflower leaves, but it was hot and nourishing to us. While Burt and I boxed, our crew and the English prisoners kept a lookout for the guards. We could not do this every morning, but we did keep it up for a few months.

The soup kettles turned out to have another use. A Polish Jewish prisoner from another crew asked me one day if I could supply electrical cable that could be used by the Polish underground for sabotage. I asked him how it could be done. He told me that when I wrote out a request for cable, I should ask for more than I needed for the day's work. I could then cut off what I did not need, put it in the empty soup kettle, and mark the lid. I sent Joe off to pick up the cable. I requested one thousand feet (305 metres), cut off three hundred feet (90 metres) to be used on the job, rolled the remaining seven hundred feet (215 metres) into the empty soup kettle, and marked the lid with a piece of chalk. Joe then returned the kettles to the side of the road to be picked up by the camp kitchen staff. But before the kettles were picked up, members of the underground came by and removed the cable. I later learned that other crews also used the kettles for getting tools and other badly needed items to the underground.

Despite strict security measures inside the works, prisoners did manage to sabotage the factory at Buna. Often, when we arrived inside the guarded section where we were supposed to work, I would be informed that the electrical power was out, and that no work could be done until the power was restored. It was my job to restore the electrical power, and to do so, I had to climb a thirty-five-foot (11 metre) wooden mast to replace the main fuses. In winter, when the mast was covered with a sheet of ice, I had to strap a pair of climbing spikes onto my shoes to climb it. This happened quite a few times, and you can be sure that the fuses did not blow by themselves. Somebody had to know exactly where to make the short circuit in order to blow them.

But aside from outright sabotage, there were other ways for prisoners to get back at the Germans. We stole from the civilians who worked in the factory, from the guards, and from the company. Every time Joe went to pick up material, he managed to come back with something he had "organized." Doing this was very dangerous. The only way to smuggle something illegal into the camp was to hide it on your body so that the guards could not see it. Anyone who was caught had to pay the penalty, usually hanging. But whatever we got our hands on was worth a bowl of soup or a piece of bread inside the camp. The block elderster often promised extra soup to anyone who could get him a certain kind of tool. And one time, as Joe was walking with his dolly, a guard called him to help unload a freight train loaded with potatoes. Joe was the right man for the job. The first thing he did was to tie up the bottom of his pant legs, and before he had finished the job, both legs of his pants were filled with potatoes that we later popped into a fire and ate!

Not long after this, Joe was caught inside the cellar where the potatoes were being stored. The guards locked him in there until he could be handed over to the *lager* ("camp") *elderster* to be punished. The lager elderster was a prisoner, usually a German, who had been interned for political reasons. He was in charge of all the prisoners in the camp and received his instructions directly from the camp commander. He was responsible for everything that happened inside the camp, and he also handed out the punishment.

As I have said, the normal punishment for stealing was a public hanging that would serve as a warning to others. Luckily, I found out where Joe was being held. I told Mr. Ritter that Joe was my brother and that I could not possibly do a good job for him knowing that my brother was about to be hanged. It worked. Mr. Ritter got Joe released, although he kicked Joe very hard in the behind and warned him to stay out of the cellar.

Joe soon got his revenge. After one of his trips to the storage rooms, he told me very quietly that he thought he had found something good. He then pulled out of his jacket a map of Europe with the battle front lines marked on it. I immediately grabbed it from him and hid it. We had our own system for hiding things from the guards. We used a pyramid shaped stack of open ended black pipe that was about five inches (thirteen centimetres) in diameter and about twenty-five feet (eight metres) long. Whatever we could get our hands on, such as tools, materials for the machines, important information like the map, and so on, we hid inside those pipes.

I knew that someone would be very interested in that map, but I also knew that it would be very dangerous if a guard found us with it. I asked Joe where on earth he had found the map, and when he told me, I nearly choked! He said that when he was wandering past Mr. Ritter's office with his dolly, he noticed that the office door was ajar and decided to take a look inside. No one was in the office, so Joe slipped inside and saw the map stuck on the wall. He figured that it might be worth some bread, so he took it. I asked him if he had any idea what would have happened to him if Ritter had caught him in the act. We've all heard about love at first sight, but between Joe and Ritter, it was hate at first sight. Every time Ritter saw Joe, he kicked him.

I showed the map to the English soldiers first. They were very interested and took it with them, promising us bread and cigarettes in return. But they brought the map back a day later. They said that it was too dangerous for them to have the map in their possession because they were searched regularly. They did bring us some bread and cigarettes though. Later, one of the English prisoners of war was hanged in the Buna camp for trying to escape. To my surprise, the other English prisoners of war did not revolt when that happened. Nor was there any protest from "Hitler's Red Cross"; they were too busy looking the other way.

I hid the map on my chest when we marched back to camp. Once we were inside the camp, we went to a barracks where we had been able to do deals before, and showed the map to the block elderster. We told him that he could have the map for only a couple of days because other block eldersters wanted to see it. When he saw what it was, he offered us both extra soup and bread for two weeks. We also traded the cigarettes that we had been given by the English prisoners for extra bread. All in all, we got good mileage out of that map.

One day inside the camp, a prisoner was assaulted by one of our guards who first roughed him up and then kicked the prisoner right between his legs. All the guards wore boots with steel plates mounted on the front of the soles and heels. This guard struck the prisoner so hard that an artery broke and blood started to run inside his crotch, which started to swell so badly that he had to remove his pants. The guard had a real good time and laughed his head off. Now the prisoner had to go to the hospital barracks. We were not allowed to help him. The swelling was getting larger by the minute. The only way for him to get to the hospital barracks by himself was to use the wheelbarrow that he used to do his work.

This is the way he started to walk to the hospital barracks. I do not know whether he got there or not. I do not remember seeing this man again.

Not long after this, I suddenly developed a very high fever and boils started to break out all over my lower body and legs. I could not work, so I was sent to the hospital barracks, called the *krankenbau,* or sick bay. The doctor, who was also a prisoner, examined me and told me that I could not stay on my feet in that condition. He told me that he would have to open up the boils, and then and there he cut them all open with a knife. It was not very pleasant and the boils started to run terribly. The doctor told me that I had to stay in the sick bay until I started to heal.

One morning while I was still in the sick bay, all the patients were called to the front of the room. We were told to stand in line naked. At the time, I had no idea who Dr. Mengele was, but I would later find out that the men who ordered us to stand there for inspection were none other than the SS selection team headed by Dr. Mengele. The SS were the Nazi storm troopers, and Dr. Mengele was to become notorious for his role in selecting prisoners for the gas chambers, and for using concentration camp prisoners for horrific medical experiments. They had come into the hospital barracks to select prisoners for transport. Once again I was selected along with other prisoners, and once again we had no idea where we were going to be taken. Then one of the prisoners, who had not been selected, said to me, "You were selected for the *kamin*." I did not understand what he meant, but someone told me later that *kamin* was the word used for the crematorium.

The Germans put us into an army truck, which then started off toward the camp gates. But just as the truck reached the gates, it was suddenly stopped by guards who called out my number and told me to get out of the truck and return to the sick bay. I had no idea what was going on, but I walked back to the hospital barracks, and when I got there, I was given some soup and bread and told to get back into bed. After a few days the wounds began to heal and I felt well enough to go back to work. First, however, I was told to report to Mr. Ritter. He told me to start work where I had left off before I got sick, and then made a remark about getting me off the truck. It turns out that Ritter had called the camp to find out when I was coming back to work, and was told that I had been put on a truck for the final trip! He was furious with the camp authorities when he heard that, and told them, "I have a crew of forty prisoners working for me on this project, and there is only one electrician amongst them. And this is the one you are taking away from me!"

Ritter had made it very clear to the camp commandant that he had been given the responsibility for getting the factory operating as soon as possible, and that his orders came directly from German military headquarters. To get the job done, he need a skilled electrician—me. The camp authorities decided not to argue with him, and that is how I got off that truck and back to work. The only film about the concentration camps I have ever watched is *Schindler's List*. My Mr. Schindler was named Obermeister Ritter.

The experience made me see Ritter in a different light. Until then I had seen him as another German bureaucrat who mindlessly followed Nazi orders and saluted "Heil Hitler." Yet he had the courage to disagree with the camp authorities, and he saved my life! Not long after this incident, he gave me some coupons that I could use in the camp store to buy "Magorka" tobacco, which he called "payment for my work." The German civilian engineers had the right to hand out coupons to those prisoners whose work was done according to their satisfaction. "Magorka" tobacco is made from the stems of tobacco leaves. Once the leaves had been stripped to prepare regular tobacco, the stems were dried and ground up. Prisoners would roll this tobacco into pieces of newspaper and smoke it. Joe and I traded the tobacco with the block elderster for some bread and soup. Every little bit extra that we could get to eat helped us stay alive a little longer.

Life in the concentration camps was unbearable for all the prisoners, but for the Dutch Jews it was impossible. In proportion to our numbers in the camps, 75 percent of Dutch Jews as compared to 90 percent of Polish Jews lost their lives. I have heard some Polish Jewish survivors say that the Dutch Jews ended up in the gas chambers much sooner than the Eastern European Jews because we did not know how to work and that we could not get used to the living conditions in the camps. My experience of this was more complicated and very difficult to write about.

It is true that I had a very hard time getting used to the abhorrent sanitary conditions in the Eastern European concentration camps. I could not bring myself to use the washroom facilities for a couple of weeks. I did not expect to see modern facilities in the concentration camps, but after the relative cleanliness of the Dutch concentration camp, the level of filth in Auschwitz came as a real shock.

Dutch Jews also suffered, however, because of their differences from Eastern European Jews. Because the Jews in Holland did not speak Yiddish, although we spoke Hebrew, the Polish Jews felt that we were not really Jewish. They taunted us because of it and refused to help us learn what we needed to know to survive in the camps. We had to find out everything the hard way. The Nazis hated us because we were Jews, while the Eastern European Jews distrusted and despised us because we weren't Jewish enough.

For example, as I mentioned, Dutch Jews did not know what the word *kamin* meant. Whenever we asked a Polish Jew, he would simply laugh and say, "*Kamin* is pffff—you go out the chimney," meaning "smoke." It took me until the end of 1944 to find out that *kamin* was the word used for "gas chamber." It is hard to avoid something if you have no idea what it is.

One of the reasons that I never volunteered my skills as an electrician is that I did not want to work for the Nazis. For me it was a form of resistance. No one had told me or any of the other Dutch Jews that letting the Germans know that we had a trade, such as plumbing, carpentry, or being an electrician, would have improved our chances of surviving longer.

When I ended up in the hospital barracks toward the end of 1944, it took me a week to find out that the German officers who forced us to strip and parade in front of them were actually Dr. Mengele and his SS gang who were doing selections for the gas chambers. The Polish Jews knew what was going on, but I did not. I suspected that I was not exactly being chosen to take a cruise on the Mediterranean, but even then the Polish Jews did not tell me what they knew.

One more incident has stayed with me through the years. The kapo, a prisoner who is in charge of a group of prisoners, could appoint a so-called foreman from among the prisoners to help supervise the work crew at the work site. One particular foreman, a Polish Jew named Itzak, decided for no apparent reason to teach me a lesson. Just as I was about to go into Mr. Ritter's office, he suddenly knocked my cap off my head and said, "You should show more respect for Mr. Ritter and remove your cap before you go inside his office." I lost my temper and landed my right fist squarely on his mouth. The temptation to turn him into pulp was enormous. As he spat out his two front teeth, I warned him never to touch me or any of my crew again. Then I calmed down and realized that I was just about to let out all my frustrations on someone who was a prisoner just like me. I told him to pick up my cap and put it back on my head, which he did. We never had any more trouble with Itzak. But the bitterness from these incidents, from our treatment by our fellow Jews, is with me still.

CHAPTER FIVE

The Death March to Dora-Nordhausen and Building the "Secret Weapon"

THE IG FARBEN FACTORY AT BUNA NEVER DID GET INTO PRODUCTION. EVERY time one of the chimneys began to smoke, it tipped off the Allies that this section of the factory was being used, and bombs would start to fall.

In late December 1944, I was once again put onto an army truck and taken to a site close to the city of Krakow, in Poland, where the Russian army was to start its offensive. It had not begun yet, but the Germans expected it at any moment. I was brought there to lay cables and install searchlights in preparation for the Russian attack. A few days later I was back in Buna again.

While I was gone, Joe was sent to the sick bay because the doctors, who were also prisoners, had discovered a swelling behind his ear and decided to operate. When I returned from Krakow, I found Joe unconscious in the sick bay.

The map that Joe had stolen from Mr. Ritter's office showed the battle fronts in the fall of 1944, so we had a pretty good idea where the fighting was taking place and how close the Russians were. That glimmer of hope had kept us alive. Soon after I returned from Krakow, we began to hear explosions in the distance, and the camp guards ordered all the prisoners to assemble in the roll-call square. Then the guards ordered all the Jews to step out of the line and gather at the side of the square. Once again my instincts told me that something was wrong. Those instincts had served me well in the past so, instead of stepping forward, I stepped backward, further into the lines. When I backed up, one of the non-Jewish prisoners said to me, "Hey, you're a Jew, you have to step out." I answered him by saying, "You open your mouth once more and you'll lose your teeth." I was considered a heavyweight among the prisoners because I weighed more than most of them, just over a hundred pounds (45 kilograms), and I could throw my "weight" around a bit. Some of the other prisoners also told this man to shut up and let me step further back through the lines.

My Star of David soon gave me away, but by then the guards had stopped looking for Jews. They must have decided that they had enough. The ones who had stepped forward were marched out of camp and the rest of us went back to the barracks. Not long after, we heard machine-gun fire and we knew the Jewish prisoners who were marched out were all dead. It turned out that the camp was about to be evacuated and there were too many prisoners to fit on the trains, so they killed the Jews. Ours was not the only camp where the Germans used this strategy; when the Allied soldiers arrived, they found many mass graves around the concentration camps.

The evacuation began about the middle of January 1945. Joe was still in the sick bay when we were ordered to start marching out of the camp. German planes were bombing some of the barracks. The Nazis were trying to destroy the barracks before the Russian troops could occupy them. They also wanted to destroy anything that could be used as evidence against them. As we were marching out of camp, I saw that the sick bay had been bombed and was on fire. At that moment, I was sure that there was no way my friend Joe could have survived.

Now the long march started. We walked for about three days through snow and ice in the bitter January cold before we reached the trains. When we left the camp, we each received a quarter loaf of bread as our food supply for the whole trip. About three thousand of us started the march, with German guards marching in front, behind, and beside us. The only consolation I had about Joe's fate was that he could not have survived this forced march. It was torture from beginning to end: anyone who slowed down was shot by the guards. The road behind us was littered with bodies.

We stopped marching when it got dark, in a place that must have been an abandoned concentration camp. We spent the night outside in the cold with no food. Some of the "big shot" prisoners, Aryans, or Germans, managed to get inside a barracks, but they made sure that none of us lowly prisoners, Jews, got inside. Wherever we marched or wherever we stopped, bodies were left behind on the road. Spending the night outside in the freezing cold was an invitation to die because, after marching all day long, you do need to have a chance to get off your feet. There was no way that I could stand up any longer. I found a spot to lie down between the dead bodies that were right around me. That way, they would block the ice-cold wind.

As soon as daylight came we had to start marching again. Finally, on the third day, we arrived at the trains. Needless to say, there was no need for first-class reservations. These were open cattle cars with no roof, no straw on the floor, no toilets, and barely room to stand. We were packed more tightly than sardines in a tin. When the car was loaded, I stood straight against the wall and could not lift my arms because of all the people pressed against me. There must have been more then two hundred people in one car alone. To make matters worse, we were forbidden to hold our heads up straight because they would be seen outside the train. Anyone who tried to look over the side of the cattle car was immediately shot by a guard who was standing in the caboose with a machine gun.

Under these conditions it did not take long before the first of the men couldn't stand any longer and fell down on their knees, and others soon collapsed. But there was no room for these men to lie down, so they died in that position. People stood on top of the bodies, and the more bodies there were, the bigger the problem became for us. It became practically impossible to keep our heads below the sides of the cattle car. A few of us decided that we would wait until dark and then throw the bodies over the side to make room for the rest of us and make it possible for us to keep our heads down.

The intolerable conditions on the train literally drove some people mad. I remember one incident with the barracks' barber (the prisoner who shaved our heads every four to six weeks). Without warning, he started to cut some of the men with a straight razor blade. There was a lot of screaming. I managed to get close enough to give him a left to the chin and he went down. Someone got the razor away from him and threw it over the side of the train. Later on the trip, the barber died.

At some point during this train ride, I noticed that the middle finger on my right hand had started to swell very badly, and that the swelling was spreading to the rest of my hand. I showed my hand to one of the prisoners who happened to be a doctor who had worked in the hospital barracks. He took one look and said, "I'm sorry. I can't help you because I have no tools or dressings. You have blood poisoning and your fingernail has to be removed. You have less than twenty-four hours to live." I didn't have much time to think about what to do.

Everyone who entered the camp had been given an aluminum bowl and soup spoon. I had reshaped the handle of my soup spoon into a knife on the grinding stone where I worked. I had done the same for some of the other prisoners, but we had to be careful that the guards didn't find out or they would have shot us for having weapons. This tool now came in very handy. I cut off my fingernail as deeply into the nail bed as I could tolerate. Then I squeezed my hand, especially the middle finger, trying to get out as much puss as I could. I took a piece of clothing from one of the bodies that was lying on the floor and cut it up to use as a dressing. Once more, I managed to escape death. My improvised surgery worked and my hand eventually healed.

When night fell, the doors opened and a guard told me and another fellow to come out. He wanted us to remove the bodies from the floor of our train car and put them outside to be stacked like a cord of wood until the floor of the train was clear. This job earned us each a piece of black bread, about another quarter of a loaf. When the job was done we had to go back inside and the door was locked again. That piece of bread was so dry that it was impossible to swallow it and I was glad when it started to snow. At least we got some snowflakes in our mouths. I cupped my hands to catch as many snowflakes as I could. Useful as the snow was to provide a few drops of water, without any protection from it we were in danger of freezing. I managed to get a piece of blanket from a dead fellow who was lying close to where I was standing and put it over my head. I think that the blanket must have carried some kind of contagious disease because I soon developed a serious problem with my eyes. But for the time being, the blanket kept me warm enough to survive. On the third day of our ordeal on the train, we arrived at our destination. The train stopped, the guards unlocked the doors, and we were told to get out. It dawned on me that the Germans still considered us to be useful to do some work and that must have been the reason for not shooting us outright with their machine guns.

When I got off the train, I was shocked to discover that, as far as I could tell, about three hundred of the more than three thousand people who had started the trip were able to walk onto the platform. The people who were still left inside the train cars couldn't walk, so the guards left them there to die. We were not allowed to help them. The rest had all perished on the trip, except for a few who had managed to escape. A sign on the station platform where we stood read "Nordhausen." That was the first time we had seen any sign that let us know where we were. In the past, wherever we had been transported, the signs had been removed to keep us all in the dark.

The Germans marched us from the train station in Nordhausen to the concentration camp in Dora, located in the middle of the Harz Mountains, in the central part of Germany, south of Berlin. Built actually inside one of the mountains was the Mittelbau factory where Hitler's "secret weapons," the v-1 and v-2 rockets, were manufactured. The Germans put these self-propelled bombs, the forerunners of both the jet engine and the intercontinental ballistic missile, on a launching track and aimed them at London, England. The bodies of these huge rockets were packed with explosives. Fortunately for London, few of the rockets ever landed in populated areas, although the ones that did land succeeded in killing about twenty-five hundred people. The rockets were not guided by radar. The direction in which they were aimed, the amount of fuel they carried, and the strength of the wind determined where they would land. This was the secret weapon that the guards and the civilians in the Buna factory were always talking about. This weapon was going to win the war for the Germans and make them a world power, although the guards did not know what this secret weapon was.

Most of the machinery that was used to manufacture the rockets, such as the electric spot welders for the large hulls of the v-2 rockets, had been confiscated from the occupied countries. I could tell that from the factory plates mounted on the frames. The machines were installed in various tunnels inside the hollowed-out mountain. Different sections of the rocket were built in each tunnel, and the workers were not allowed to go into any tunnel other than the one they were assigned to. That way, none of the workers could know everything about the design the manufacturing of these rockets because this was top secret.

I was told that I would be joining a group of electricians who maintained and repaired the machinery inside the factory. But when I reported to the kapo of the electrical crew, he took one look at the Star of David sewn on the left side of my prison jacket and said, "You're a Jew. I have only

German Aryan people like myself in my crew; I won't allow a Jew in my crew." He was overruled, however, because the camp commander ordered him to accept me. He was furious and swore that he would find another way to get rid of me. He promised that he would finish me off within three weeks, and he did his best to keep his word. He was as mean as they come. My electrical crew worked the night shift, and my "friend" the kapo worked me over every night with his rubber hose.

Needless to say, the Nazis were very concerned about sabotage of their secret project. Every morning, as the prisoners were marched out of the mountain through the exit tunnel, the guards forced us to watch a show of brutality as a warning of what would happen to us if we ever tried to sabotage the works. At the exit, there was a crane that was used to lift the rockets onto a flatbed train, then they were covered with a green tarp. When the rockets were being transported to their launching pad they were not yet loaded with fuel or explosives. Often, as soon as the train moved out of the tunnel, delta-wing-shaped airplanes would swoop down and machine-gun the train and its deadly cargo. The rockets would then have to be moved back into the tunnel for repairs.

But the Germans had another use for the crane: as a gallows to hang prisoners who were accused of sabotage. If a civilian worker or scientist pointed out any prisoner to a guard and accused him of sabotage, that prisoner would be next in line for the crane, no questions asked. About eight prisoners would be lined up, each one with his hands tied behind his back, a rope tied around his neck, and a small stick in his mouth that was held in place by two strings knotted behind his head. The stick was there to stop the sound of the screams as the crane slowly pulled the prisoners up by the ropes around their necks. We had to stand there and watch. The civilian workers were also allowed to watch, and one day, two young German girls stood right in front of me watching as the crane pulled up several prisoners. Just then a third girl joined the other two, who said to her, "You came just in time. If you had arrived a little later, it would have been all over and you would have missed the part when they kick their legs." They thought that it was fun to watch the prisoners die. I assume that the girls were secretaries. After the war they probably swore that they knew nothing about what happened in the concentration camps.

Yet, in spite of the threat of this horrific penalty, there was still sabotage inside the mountain. For example, one night I was ordered to check a large electric motor that was defective. After taking it apart, I saw that the motor winding had been cut with a hacksaw. There was no way to repair this kind of damage. One of the German civilian workers who saw the damage was sure that it was the work of one of the Russian prisoners.

In fact, all the people who worked on the v-1 and v-2 rocket project, including the rocket scientists Wernher von Braun and Arthur Rudolph, were either civilians or prisoners; I never saw any high-ranking German officers. There were no military personnel at the Dora-Mittelbau works above the rank of guard. In other words, the decision to hang prisoners at this factory deep inside the Harz Mountains must have been made by civilians alone; these were not orders given by German army officers. And the top civilian in charge of the Mittelbau factory was the rocket scientist Arthur Rudolph, the same man who would later be brought to the United States by the U.S. government as part of "Project Paperclip," along with other scientists and engineers recruited for the American rocket programs. As part of this post-war project, Rudolph headed the Saturn V rocket program that carried U.S. astronauts to the moon.

Coincidentally, as I wrote this section of the book, on May 3, 1993, a radio newscast announced that Arthur Rudolph had been denied a Canadian hearing in a bid to gain re-entry to the United States. Despite having been recruited by the U.S. government after the war, in 1982 Rudolph was ordered out of the country and his American citizenship was revoked because of war crimes. He was attempting to get permission to go back to the U.S., and had asked for a hearing in Canada so that his daughter, who was still living in the U.S., would be able to testify on his behalf. I was especially interested in these hearings against Rudolph because, as far as I knew, there were no other concentration camp survivors in Canada who could testify about what happened at the Mittelbau factory.

According to Rudolph's testimony, the prisoners who worked on the v-1 and v-2 rockets had nothing to complain about and were treated very well. He never once mentioned the beatings and hangings that took place inside the mountain on a daily basis. When I heard this, I called the Simon Wiesenthal Center, which promptly arranged a meeting between a court reporter and myself in their Toronto office. I recorded testimony for the hearing about the treatment of the prisoners who worked on the v-1 and v-2 rockets. In the end, a Canadian Immigration Department adjudicator ordered Rudolph out of Canada because of his complicity in war crimes and crimes against humanity. Rudolph returned to Germany, where he lived until his death in 1996.

But this was to come much later. While I was still working in Mittelbau, the kapo of my electrical crew never let up on me. The beatings continued every night, and I knew that if I lifted so much as a finger against him, the guards would shoot me without any hesitation. Nonetheless, the night came that I could not take anymore. As I was working on a motor part on the floor, the kapo came up behind me and hit me in the neck with his rubber hose. I got up, turned around, and ran away through the tunnel. I found a door and barged right in. I'll never forget the stunned look on the faces of about fifteen civilian engineers who were sitting around a long table. I had just crashed a meeting of rocket scientists, and there was no time to formally introduce myself. Here I was, dressed in prison garb, with my head shaved, filthy, bleeding, and bruised all over, and right behind me was the kapo, who had followed me, still holding his rubber hose.

One of the engineers regained his composure and began firing questions at us. "What the hell are you doing here?" he asked. The language was probably a little rougher, but I think you get the idea. By this time I could speak German fluently, so I pointed at the kapo and said, "He won't let me work. He beats me up all the time." I figured that if I was a goner, I might as well try to take the kapo down with me. I kept repeating the same words over and over because I didn't know what else to say. The scientists told me to shut up and started to question the kapo. "What is the story here?" they asked. The kapo replied, "He's a Jew and he pretends to be an electrician. As you well know, that's not possible." The engineer in charge asked the kapo if he was an electrician. The kapo answered that he was not, but that he was in charge of the electrical work crew. The engineer then asked him, "If you're not an electrician, how could you possibly judge if the Jew is an electrician?" He turned to the others and said, "This is a clear case of sabotage. If this Jew is not an electrician, then he committed sabotage by claiming to be one, and will be hanged in the morning. Let's give him a test right here and now. If he proves to be an electrician, then the kapo is the one who committed the sabotage and he will be hanged in the morning." Somehow, on the spur of the moment, I had used exactly the right words to get their attention. Security and secrecy may have been high on their list of worries, but sabotage was their biggest concern of all.

The scientists put me in front of a large wooden panel that was mounted on the wall, and on the panel was a whole arrangement of wires, switches, connecting strips, and electrical clips. They then told me to make certain connections. Several of the other engineers joined in the demonstration and asked me to perform other switching tasks. It didn't take more than fifteen minutes to prove that I knew my stuff. The scientists told me to go back to my job. In the morning as we were marching out of the tunnel, the crane had again been pressed into service as a gallows, hanging prisoners who were accused of committing sabotage. Only this time, my kapo was one of them.

During my time in Dora-Mittelbau, the problem with my eyes that had started on the train was getting worse and worse. My eyes were becoming increasingly sensitive to light. Any bright light, whether it was electric light or sunlight, would cause them to close up and I had a hard time getting them to open again. In the factory I managed to "organize," that is, I managed to get my hands on, a pair of welder's glasses. They really helped because they blocked my eyes from light, and it was actually easier for me to see in the dark. I know that this sounds contradictory, but I felt better in the dark than in the daylight. So working in the night shift was much easier for me than working in the daytime. By this time, my eyes would not function in daylight at all.

CHAPTER SIX

Liberation

AT THE BEGINNING OF APRIL 1945, EVERYTHING CHANGED. THE FIRST HINT we got was that one night, without any explanation, we were not taken to work our regular shift at the factory. The next morning, all the German guards had disappeared from the camp, and in their place were Hungarian guards. The German guards had fled because they knew that when the Allied troops arrived, the Germans would be held responsible for the deplorable conditions and horrific events in the camp. All the prisoners were kept inside the camp. We no longer went into the mountain to work. Rumours were flying around that there were liberating troops nearby. We could hear bombs exploding and machine gun fire that sounded not far off.

And then it was over. The Hungarian guards surrounding the camp put white flags on their rifles and the first Allied troops walked into the concentration camp to liberate us. I was free after more than three years in captivity. The date was April 13, 1945.

I have often been asked how it felt when I first realized that we were finally being liberated from the terror and the torture that we had lived with for so long. My first feeling was disbelief. I could hardly believe that it was really over. When the reality sank in, the disbelief was followed by a strange sensation that I can best describe as feeling like a flat tire after all the air pressure had been drained out of it. The one feeling I never had was jubilation because I had a strong feeling that I was the only survivor in my family. I knew that my wife, my parents, my sisters, and my nephew could not possibly have survived the Nazi's senseless, brutal, and deliberate destruction of human life.

When the first Allied soldiers marched into the camp, I thought that they were English because by then my eyes were so badly infected that I could barely see anything. I couldn't even see my liberators. Forty-seven years later, in May 1992, I found out that the liberating troops were Americans: the 3rd Armored Division, 140th Infantry. According to Rabbi Gunther Plaut, who was with the U.S. troops, those soldiers could not believe their eyes. Nothing had prepared them for what they saw—skeletons everywhere, some of whom could still move a little and some of whom could walk.

The soldiers started to hand out tinned food. We did not have any can openers, but we attacked the tins with spoons and any other tool that we could find. Handing out the food like that was actually a big mistake, because quite a few of us started to eat whatever was inside of the tins, ham, corned beef, or beans, including the fat. But our weakened bodies could not digest such rich food. Many of the prisoners got terrible cramps and some died from eating too much, too soon. I ate whatever I could get my hands on, but fortunately, I mostly ate bread.

As soon as possible, the American commander started trying to sort out the survivors. He gathered as much information as he could and then grouped us together according to what country we came from. There were 102 Dutch survivors in the Dora camp. The commander decided to transport those of us who were in the worst physical shape back to Holland on army trucks. Since I was one of the skeletons who could still walk, I was allowed to sit up front beside the driver. I must have been quite a sight. I weighed all of eighty-five pounds (thirty-nine kilograms) and wore welder's glasses.

After several hours on the road, our driver decided to stop at a farm house to see if there was any food there. He came out with a small ceramic bowl that he handed to me and said, "Wet your fingers in your mouth, stick them in the bowl, and then lick your fingers." The bowl was full of sugar. It tasted delicious! Then I felt something else inside the bowl. I took it out and saw that it was a wristwatch. I showed it to the driver and said in my best English, "I'll make you a deal. You keep the watch and I'll keep the sugar." At that moment, the sugar was worth much more to me than the watch.

Getting to the Dutch border was like driving an obstacle course. The roads, railways, and bridges had all been destroyed. Everything was in chaos. The army trucks managed to get through, though, and they delivered us to the Philips Hospital in Eindhoven, Holland. As soon as we arrived, the hospital staff cleaned us up and put us to bed. It felt very strange. A bed with a white sheet and blankets for us? They were also very careful not to serve us any solid foods, just soup and other liquids.

Not long after our arrival, a woman walked into our ward and welcomed us back with an armful of flowers. She told us that she represented the Red Cross. We asked her if we could eat the flowers, and, if we couldn't, to leave us alone and take the flowers with her! After what we had been through, the name of the Red Cross left a bad taste in our mouths. We could still hear their deafening silence while we were being murdered and tortured in the Nazi concentration camps. It is now fifty years later, and I am still very bitter about the way the organization behaved during World War II.

We were closely monitored by the doctors in Eindhoven for several weeks. I was in the hospital for about two months. None of the medical staff had ever seen anything like my eye condition before, but they did find a way to treat it. Slowly I started to improve. Later on, we were told by a panel of doctors that we would all have to face the fact that we had lost at least twenty years of our normal life span because of the way we had lived in the concentration camps. We really had something to look forward to!

While I was still in the hospital, we were visited by several representatives of both the Dutch government and the Red Cross. One of them, a young man with a briefcase, walked into our ward and told us that he was doing a survey for the Dutch government regarding those who were arrested during the war for doing resistance work, or who were connected with the underground movement and had survived. When he got to me, I explained some of the things I had done in Holland and in the camps. He stopped me right in the middle and said, "Are you a Jew?" I said yes. "Oh," he said, in quite a derogatory way, "then it doesn't count." As he got up to leave, I said, "Hitler himself could not have said it better than you just did."

Soon after that, members of the Red Cross came to the hospital and collected the names of concentration camp survivors. As I suspected, there was no record of any survivors from my family. But I still remembered my pact with Max Pels to look after his family, and I was anxious to start looking for his children, Katy and Philip. I asked the officials if they could find out where the children were. It was time to find what family I had left.

CHAPTER SEVEN

Finding the Children

MY FIRST PROMISING LEAD IN THE SEARCH FOR KATY AND PHILIP CAME through the Dutch Red Cross. I found the names of two children on their list, Katy and Philip Pelsma, who were the same ages as the children I was looking for. I was anxious to check out this lead, but there was something I had to do first.

As soon as I was strong enough to travel, I left the hospital in Eindhoven and travelled to Amsterdam by the one available means of transportation, hitching a ride on an army truck. I was wearing all my possessions: an old pair of army pants that an American soldier had given me, a shirt from the hospital, and my welder's glasses. When I arrived in Amsterdam, I went straight to the house where I had lived with my family.

I wanted to get the photographs and identity cards that I had hidden inside the wall of our flat. When I showed up at the door, the woman who now lived there became abusive. I explained that I just wanted to get my family papers back, but she threatened me with the police if I didn't leave immediately. I backed off right away, because, believe me, the last thing I wanted to see was another uniform!

I wasn't sure what to do next, so I went back down the stairs and sat on the steps of Mr. Biermasz's laboratory across the street from my old house. That was where and when I realized that I was the only survivor of my entire family. It was time to face reality. While I was sitting there, planning my next move, a man walking by suddenly stopped and said, "Aren't you Mike?" I looked up and saw Bernard Ossendrijver, who was related to my oldest sister, Esther, by marriage. He asked me what I was doing in front of my house, and I explained what had happened. He warned me that the people living in the house had been put there in 1943 by the Nazis, so they must have been Nazi sympathizers. He advised me not to stir up any trouble and to leave them alone. He asked if I had any place to sleep and any ration coupons for food. I told him that I did not have a place to sleep and I didn't know anything about the ration coupons because, until then, I had been in the hospital. He told me that all I had to do to get the coupons was to notify the government registration office that I was back in Amsterdam and needed my food rations. It sounded simple enough.

I should have known that it would not be that easy. When I got to the government office, the officials wouldn't give me any coupons because, according to them, I was dead and, therefore, did not need food coupons. I asked the clerk if he had ever talked to a dead person, and when he said no, I told him that he was in the process of doing so right now! I asked him where I had supposedly died. He replied that I had been shot during the fighting in the Waterlooplein Square in Amsterdam in the spring of 1941. If I really was Michel Engelschman, I had to prove it by getting two non-Jewish people to testify on my behalf.

Fortunately, I was able to find two people to do so. One of them was a plumber named Mr. Van Rijn, who was more than willing to identify me. He had also kept all of my electrical tools for me during the war and returned them to me. Even with his testimony, it took about three weeks before I finally got my food ration coupons. In the meantime, the government officials gave me a few coupons to tide me over.

Throughout this time, the Red Cross kept updating the list of survivors, but having spent more than two years in the concentration camps, and having seen so many Dutch Jews die, I knew that the lists would not be very long. In my heart, I knew that, with the possible exception of my sister Duifje, my family had not survived. I thought that Duifje might possibly have survived because of her physical strength—she had worked on farms and was trained for work on a kibbutz in Israel—and because of her ability to speak several languages. However, that hope proved to be in vain.

My eyes were still not healing very well, and I could go outside only when the sun wasn't shining. I had managed to hang on to the welder's glasses that I had "organized" in Mittelbau and, when I used them, I could

The laboratory across from our old house

keep my eyes open a little on cloudy days. Light from a twenty-five watt bulb inside at night would force my eyes closed, so I even wore the welder's glasses inside the house.

Despite the problem with my eyes, however, I was starting to get restless and to feel strong enough to travel to Limburg to look for Katy and Philip. As I have already mentioned, travelling then was not easy. The roads, railway tracks, and bridges had all been blown up, and army trucks remained the sole means of transportation. Still wearing my old pair of army pants, my hospital shirt, and my welder's goggles, I stuck out my thumb and asked for rides from any army trucks that were going my way.

When I got to Limburg, I found the address that the Red Cross had given me, in the village of Spekholzerheide, at that time a twenty-minute streetcar ride to the German border. The house belonged to Anna and Drago Mandic. The front of the house was a butcher shop, with an apartment in the back, and bedrooms on the second floor.

I knocked on the door, and it was opened by a young girl who was about eighteen years old. Her name was Ennie, and she was Mrs. Mandic's niece. When I told Ennie why I was there, she went back into the apartment to get her aunt. I explained to Mrs. Mandic who I was. I told her that my sister, Esther, was related to the children's parents by marriage, and that the two families had lived in the same house in Amsterdam. While I was talking to her, I could see the children standing right there.

Katy was seven years old, and although she had been three and a half years of age the last time she saw me, she recognized me right away and ran straight into my arms. That was proof enough for Mrs. Mandic. She invited me inside and asked me to stay until her husband, Drago, came home from the coal mine where he worked. Philip was there too, but he had been a year and a half old the last time he saw me, so he didn't recognize me and hung back a little.

When Rika had decided that Katy and Philip should be taken out of Amsterdam and hidden in the Dutch countryside, early in the winter of 1942, the Dutch underground had contacted the Mandics and asked if they would take care of two little children whose parents had been killed during the bombardment of Rotterdam. The Mandics had agreed. Soon after Katy and Philip arrived, they realized that these were Jewish children, but Anna and Drago, two devout Catholics, decided to protect their foster children with their lives. And that is exactly what they did.

Anna Mandic was born in Germany, and her husband, Drago was born in Yugoslavia, but both had moved to Holland when they were very young, and both became Dutch citizens. As an adult, Drago worked in the coal mines in the southern part of Limburg. In the last year of the war, Anna became ill and her niece, Ennie Jansen, moved into their house to help Anna with the daily chores and to help look after Katy and Philip.

Now that Anna and Drago knew who I was, they offered me a bed for the night. In fact, I ended up staying with them for several days. Less than a week after my arrival, there was another knock on the front door and when it was opened, who should be standing there, but Rika Pels, the children's mother!

Katy and Philip with their foster mother and Ennie, c. 1943

Rika and her husband, Max, had been arrested in Amsterdam early in 1944. Two Dutch people, Ans Van Dijk and Simon Van Hoorn, had sold them out to the Nazis for money. After the war, Ans Van Dijk had the dubious honour of being the only woman in Holland ordered by the Dutch courts to be executed for war crimes. Simon Van Hoorn was jailed for his crimes against Jews during the war.

Soon after Rika and Max were arrested, they were sent to the transit camp in Westerbork. From there, they were put on a transport train to Auschwitz-Birkenau. Rika was then moved from Birkenau to a slave labour camp in Willishtal and Sarvenstein to work in a weapons factory for a couple of months. After that she was taken to the concentration camp in Theresienstadt, where she was liberated in the spring of 1945.

After the liberation, Rika had travelled from Theresienstadt by train to the city of Maastricht in the Dutch province of Limburg. Posted on the platform of the train station was a list of the names of the children who were hidden in the southern part of Limburg. Katy and Philip's names were on that list. Rika left the train station immediately and managed to get a ride to the Mandics' house in an army jeep driven by an American soldier. She knocked on their door and introduced herself to Anna and Drago as Katy and Philip's mother.

Until Rika walked into the Mandics' house, I had not even known that she had survived. Her hair was still cut very short in a crew cut and she weighed about 110 pounds (50 kilograms). Katy recognized Rika as her mother, but she kept a bit of a distance. She could not understand what had happened to her mother's curly hair. Rika could see that the two children were a little nervous around her. To help put them at ease, she pulled out of her purse a chocolate bar that the American soldier had given her and offered Katy and Philip each a piece. They had never tasted chocolate because of rationing during the war. After Philip had finished his piece of chocolate, he went outside to play, but he came back in almost immediately and, pulling on Rika's skirt, he said, "Lady, could I please have another piece of chocolate?" His sister Katy, ever the diplomat, said, "Stupid, this isn't a lady, this is your mother." But that did not make any sense to Philip. He had been a baby when he last saw Rika, and he could not understand that this skinny lady with no hair was supposed to be his mother when Anna, the woman he knew as his mother, was standing right there.

Rika and I saw that it would take some time for the children to get used to us, and that the thought of being separated from them was very painful for the Mandics. The four adults together decided that Rika and I would start off by staying with Anna and Drago and the children for about a week or so. After that, Rika and I would return to Amsterdam and leave the children with their foster parents until we could find a place to live. The plan was that we would bring Katy and Philip and the Mandics to stay with us in Amsterdam for a few weeks. At the end of the visit, the four of them, Anna, Drago, Katy, and Philip, would go back to stay in Limburg for a few weeks. We would let the children go back and forth as many times as it took for them to get used to living with Rika and me and to living in the city.

When I was back in Amsterdam, I went to the laboratory across the street from my old house and found the Biermasz family still living there. I remembered that before my family was rounded up, my father had told me that he had given Mr. Biermasz some money to keep for us, so that if any members of our family returned after the war, we could use this money to start over again. I asked Mr. Biermasz for some of the money, and I left the rest with him in case any other members of my family returned.

Rika and I decided to stay together. In our hearts, we were sure that Yettie and Max had not survived. This was confirmed by other survivors, who had known them in the camps. Being the lone survivors from both of our families formed a bond between us and brought us closer together. In September 1945 we found a place to live in Amsterdam. We were anxious to get back to Limburg right away to pick up the children and their foster parents. However, this was easier said than done. The train took us part of the way, and the rest of the trip still had to be made by getting rides in army trucks.

The first time that Rika and I went back to Limburg from Amsterdam, we were picked up by an army truck belonging to the Jewish army from Palestine, which had set up camp nearby. It so happened that they picked us up on a Friday afternoon. The driver of the truck informed his commander that he had two Jewish concentration camp survivors in his truck. The Jewish commander, Baron de Rothschild, invited us to Sabbath dinner. It was quite an experience. Rika sat beside the commander at the head of the table. He said the Kiddush and the blessing over the bread. And then we were served dinner by German prisoners, men and women who were former concentration camp guards. Can you imagine what it was like for us to be served dinner by the same people who a short time ago had tried to destroy us?

That night we slept in a tent that Commander Rothschild ordered the German prisoners to set up for us. We felt like royalty. In the morning, after breakfast, the army unit drove us as far as they could. From that point, we were able to take a train to Limburg.

After a while, we had established a routine of visiting Limburg for a couple of weeks at a time, staying with the Mandics and the children, and then leaving the children with their foster parents for several weeks. Then the Mandics would bring the children to Amsterdam and all four of them would stay with us.

Slowly the children got used to being with us, and eventually they came to live with us in Amsterdam permanently. They knew that any time they wished, they could go back to Limburg to see their foster parents. Sadly though, Anna Mandic died less than a year after the end of the war. Drago Mandic died in an accident in the coal mine several years later, in November of 1956, after we had already moved to Canada. Our children mourned them when they heard about both deaths. They loved these people dearly.

Rika and I set up our household with the children in November 1945. We had given the children time to get used to living with us, but the process of starting this new family also forced me to accept a new life with a new direction. For the first time since my return from the camps, I had a mental road map for the future. I may not have anticipated all the forks in the road and the unmarked road crossings, but I have never regretted following this path, and would do it again without hesitation.

For one thing, looking after my new family left me with no time to dwell on my own pain. The horrors of the concentration camps and the grief of losing my parents, my sisters, and my wife, were and still are, always with me.

I had experienced my most devastating moment of utter loneliness when I came back to Amsterdam and sat on the steps of the Biermasz laboratory across the street from the house where I had lived, the house that I was no longer allowed to enter. At that moment, I did not feel at all thankful that I had survived the Holocaust, knowing that I was the sole survivor in my family. But all that began to change as I watched my new family doing ordinary everyday things like Rika cooking and the children going to school.

The children also began to settle in and accept us as a family. I remember one evening when the four of us were having dinner in our apartment. I don't remember exactly what Rika and I were discussing, but I told Rika that I disagreed with something that she had said. Philip, who was all of five years old, told me that if I didn't agree with his mother, then I should go away. I winked at Rika and said that I thought this was a very good idea. I stood up and got my coat from the hallway. As I pretended to leave the apartment, Philip called out to me, "Wait a minute, I have to get my jacket. I'm coming with you."

Katy was doing well too. The summer after we had all moved to Amsterdam to stay, the Danish government offered all Dutch children above a certain age who were war victims a free three-month vacation in Denmark. Katy qualified, and we decided to let her go. When she came back, she looked like a toasted Danish and talked double Dutch; that is, she looked good, but her Dutch was a little scrambled.

In 1945, the last thing on my mind was religion. After witnessing such unspeakable crimes in the camps, how could I believe in a higher being? The children had spent the war living with the Mandics as Catholics, and Rika and I had no heart then for religion of any kind. That would change much later, in Canada in 1955, when Katy was beginning a serious relationship with her future husband, Danny Brass. Thinking about the possibility of Katy's marriage and the possibility of grandchildren made me realize that the Holocaust had robbed me not only of my family, but also of my religion. This, I decided then, was something I could change. Fifteen years after our liberation from the camps, Rika and I joined a Conservative synagogue and returned to the Jewish religion. But, when we first began our new life together, we were content to fill every day with the ordinary details of family and survival.

CHAPTER EIGHT

Picking Up the Pieces

WHILE MY FAMILY WAS SETTLING INTO OUR NEW LIFE IN AMSTERDAM, I managed to find out where my friend Ado Broodboom was living. It was not easy to track him down. He'd spent most of the war on the road with the band, travelling all over Holland. In 1944 he'd married Melly Sudy, who sang in several bands, including the one Ado played with. They travelled and played together until the end of the war. After the liberation of Holland, the band went on the road again. They made a grand tour through the country to honour the Canadian liberators. In 1946 they played in Switzerland, and in 1947 they travelled by army truck to perform in Spain.

Fortunately, when I went looking for him, Ado was in Amsterdam. The people living at his old address were able to tell me where he had moved. He was living on the third floor of a house. I rang the outside bell and somebody opened the door from the top of the stairwell. I called up, "Is Ado in?" And then I heard Ado's voice reply, "It's about time you picked up your watch. It has been ready for a long time!" The watch he was referring to was the same watch that I had asked him to take in for repairs before Yettie and I were arrested in 1943. His greeting tells you a lot about who Ado is.

After I had been back in Amsterdam for a few months, I also ran into someone who told me that he had just spoken to Joe De Jong. I told him in no uncertain terms that he must be crazy. I had practically seen Joe die before my very eyes in the burning sick bay that was bombed by the Germans when we evacuated the Buna camp. I had no doubt whatsoever that this man must be talking about somebody else. Still, I gave him my address and told my friend to bring the man over. Imagine my shock when the very next day he walked in with Joe. I thought I was seeing a ghost. Joe had brought his wife, Lineke, with him. She had also survived the concentration camps. The four of us, Joe, Lineke, Rika, and I, became best friends.

Joe told us the story of how he had been saved from the fire by the Russian army. He had been knocked out in the bombing, but two other patients had picked him up and carried him to another barracks. The Russians, who had arrived in the camp while the barracks were still burning, found Joe unconscious, but alive, and took him to Odessa, in Russia. After he had recuperated, the Russians had put him on a freight ship and sent him back to Holland.

Joe had news about another Dutch survivor from the Buna camp. When Joe had the job of picking up electrical cable and supplies from the storage room at Buna, he was given his supplies by another Dutchman named Baby Prins. Baby let Joe know that he had a pretty good idea what Joe was doing with all the extra cable. Joe had promised that if Baby agreed to look the other way, he would give him a loaf of bread. When Joe and I were reunited in Amsterdam, he told me that Baby Prins was in a hospital there. We both went to visit him and brought him a loaf of bread. A promise is a promise!

During this whole time, my eyes continued to give me trouble. I had to go through an elaborate ritual just to get them open in the morning. First, I put ice-cold compresses on my eyelids. When I was finally able to open my eyes, the eyeballs were rolled back in their sockets. Before I could see anything at all, I had to wait for the pupils to come forward again. At that point my vision was actually quite good, but, as I have described, it was an ordeal. An eye specialist in Amsterdam sent me to a university clinic in the city of Utrecht where they specialized in eye problems. After doing a lot of tests, the doctors finally told me that my eyes could be cured, but the treatment might take up to two years. They prescribed electric shock treatment at a special clinic in Amsterdam. At the clinic they also massaged my eyes, which was very helpful, but I went through almost two years of electric shock treatment twice a week before I was able to open my eyes in a normal way.

Just a few years ago, I read an article in the *Toronto Star* that described this eye condition. I learned that it is called blepharospasm. People who suffer from it are usually declared functionally blind. Fortunately for me, the electric shock treatment that I received did work and my eyes improved tremendously. I was able to start doing electrical work again, so I rented part of a basement from a sign painter and set up a small workshop. I got around the city to my various jobs on a motorbike. Katy and Philip loved to ride with me. I also began an electronics technician's course, and got my diploma two years later.

In 1948 the Dutch government issued death certificates for those who had not returned from the concentration camps. This meant that Rika and I were legally free to marry. On February 10, 1949, Hendrika Pels and Michel Engelschman were married. Now it really was time to think about the future.

Although I was very saddened by the loss of my whole family, I knew I had to move on. I had made up my mind to move ahead and start a new life with Rika and her children and move to a new country to start anew. This was not an easy thing to do.

Rika and I realized that we could not stay in Holland. There were too many bad memories. Every street in our neighbourhood reminded us of a relative who had never returned from the concentration camps. In early 1950, the Australian consulate ran an advertisement in one of the Dutch newspapers asking for carpenters, plumbers, and electricians who were willing to emigrate to Australia. They were offering tradesmen a very good deal. If I remember correctly, the Australian government would pay part of the cost of the trip if the prospective immigrant had participated in the resistance movement. As an electrical contractor and troubleshooter in Holland after the war, I did a lot of work for companies that owned buildings in Amsterdam, as well as work for building contractors and renovators. One of these contractors was a man named Vitalie.

Mr. Vitalie decided to take the Australians up on their proposal, together with some of the people who worked for him. He asked me if I was interested in joining them, and he also offered me a very good deal.

I was very interested in Mr. Vitalie's proposition, but Rika did not want to go because she thought that Australia was too far away. She said that "it wasn't exactly next door." And, although I had no problem qualifying for immigration, the Australian government set one last condition. They wanted to interview my wife separately. During her private interview, Rika let them know that she was not very keen on the idea of moving to Australia. So much for that plan! Aside from Rika's reluctance, I had

Wedding photo of Hendrika and Michael, February 10, 1949

another reason not to go. My friend Joe said that he also wanted to emigrate, but, because he was a furrier by trade, he would not have any way of making a living in Australia. He asked us if we would consider emigrating to a country where he could use his trade.

A short time after our discussion, another advertisement for tradespeople appeared in the newspaper, this time from the Canadian consulate. Rika decided that Canada could be considered next door to Holland, and, with her consent, I applied for Canadian papers. It wasn't too difficult because I already had papers from the Australian consulate. In a very short time, Rika, Katy, Philip, and I received our papers to emigrate to Canada. I promised Joe and his family that as soon as I had a steady job, I would sponsor him. I kept my promise. Six months after I started working for the Toronto Television Company, Joe, Lineke, and their daughter, Fietje, also emigrated to Canada.

In April 1952, our new family left Holland from the Port of Rotterdam on a cruise ship, the *Nieuw Amsterdam,* sailing to New York en route to Canada. On board this ship was a Jewish jeweller and his wife from New York, who fell in love with our daughter, Katy. They only had sons and very much wanted a daughter. They actually offered us money to let Katy go to live with them in New York. They told us that, as immigrants, we had a difficult time ahead of us and that Katy would have a much better life with them because of all they could offer her. Rika was furious. I was too, but my thoughts were a little different. I could see myself picking up this man, throwing him over the railing, and then yelling, "Man overboard!" Fortunately, we managed to control ourselves and politely declined. We were off on a new adventure with our family intact.

CHAPTER NINE

Canada, Here We Come!

AS SOON AS WE ARRIVED IN NEW YORK, I KNEW THAT I COULD NEVER LIVE in a city like that. It was completely overwhelming. Coming from a small country like Holland, I found walking between the huge skyscrapers to be awe-inspiring, but strangely unpleasant. And our first experience there didn't help. When we walked off the ship we asked a cab driver where the cargo office was. He offered to take us there and, after a fifteen-minute drive, he let us off and told us that the fare was twenty dollars. That the fare was so high was bad enough, but when I looked around at the place he had dropped us, I discovered that the ship was actually a five-minute walk from the cargo office! That was our welcome to New York City.

We stayed in New York for about a week at the New Yorker Hotel. Then we travelled by train to Toronto, crossing the border into Canada at Niagara Falls.

The immigration officer who took our passports at the border asked me how I pronounced my name and what it meant. I explained that in Dutch, my name meant "Englishman." He promptly added the English spelling to my passport and told me that, from then on, I could legally spell my name either way. When we first arrived in Canada, we used both Dutch and English spellings, and then gradually, with the exception of writing to people in Holland, we got used to using the English spelling.

Not long after our border crossing, we arrived at Union Station in Toronto, the end of the line and the end of our journey. At the time, Toronto was our destination because that was where the shipping company was sending our luggage and the crate with the rest of our belongings. We had arrived without any place to stay, and our first priority was to find somewhere to live.

Rika and I sat in the station's massive lobby, trying to read the newspaper so that we could find a flat to rent. We had a very hard time reading a newspaper in a strange language with all the abbreviations in the "For rent" columns. The small amount of English that we knew was not even enough to find our way to the washrooms.

In the coffee shop, when we asked a waitress for the washrooms, her reply was, "If it is not on the menu today, we will serve it tomorrow." But we had to find a place to live, and while Rika and I tried to make sense out of the classified ads, Katy and Philip decided to scout around a bit. They soon came back and showed us silver coins that they had found in the coin return slots of the pay telephones. "Look at that," I said. "We've just arrived and already you children are making money. No wonder they say 'Go to America.' You can find money lying in the streets."

Rika and I went back to our struggle with the newspaper, but a few minutes later we were very relieved to see a familiar face. We had known Abraham Hes in Holland. His wife, Hetty, had been in the camp in Theresienstadt with Rika, and they had become friends. Abe, as we called him, had heard that we were coming to Canada and that we had sailed on the *Nieuw Amsterdam,* so he had come to Union Station every time a train arrived from New York to see if we were on it.

He knew that we needed a place to live and thought that there might be a place for rent on the street where he lived. He offered to take us home with him to check it out. He was right about the place for rent, and we found our first Canadian home in a flat at 341 Markham Street in downtown Toronto, on the same day that we arrived. The flat was on the second floor of a house, with a kitchen and three other rooms. Luckily, the flat was at least partly furnished with some furniture, pots and pans, cutlery, and dishes, because as it turned out, our belongings had not arrived yet. In fact, our luggage and the crate did not arrive until three weeks later. We stayed in that flat on Markham Street for less than two months, but finding it so quickly helped us get settled into our new life in Canada.

I started looking for work as an electrician right away, but everywhere I went, I was told that, being an immigrant, I would have to start out as an apprentice, which meant that I had to work under supervision. Since I was already an experienced electrician, I considered that an insult. I was also told that in order to work, I would have to join the electricians' union. All together, I found the prospects very unappealing, so I decided to look for another kind of job.

After about two weeks of looking, I was offered a job with the Toronto Television Company, and I took it. I had gotten my diploma in basic electronics before I left Holland, but I had never worked in the field. Still, I preferred starting out in this new field to going back to being an apprentice electrician and being forced to join the union. The salary was good for the time, eighty cents an hour, although I did not get any extra pay for overtime. In 1952 there were no standard wages in the industry. Television technology was still very new and I felt lucky to be able to start somewhere.

My first job at the company wasn't exactly the most important work. I painted the long element bars for television roof antennas with aluminum paint. All I had to do was to put a bunch of the bars into a trough filled with aluminum paint, and then take them out to dry. But at least I looked important. Because our baggage hadn't arrived yet I did the work in a three hundred dollar tailor-made suit. I simply had nothing else to wear! Just before leaving Holland, I had this suit made for the start of my new life in Canada. Like almost everything else in Europe right after the war, the material for the suit could only be bought on the black market. That's what made it so expensive. Fortunately, though, it didn't take the company long to offer me other work.

One day I was watching one of the other workers using a drill press to drill some holes in a piece of metal, and when I heard how much noise the machine was making, I started to laugh. The shop foreman asked me why I was laughing. I told him that, in Holland, we usually didn't drill holes with a coffee grinder! I explained that the machine was so noisy because it was badly in need of repair. The foreman asked if I knew what was wrong with it and if I could repair it. I told him that if he would lend me some tools, I could fix the machine. He gave me the tools and pretty soon I had the machine purring like a cat with a wet nose. After they saw what I could do, the company put me in charge of the maintenance of all the machines in the workshop and raised my salary to eighty-five cents an hour. I was on my way up.

Soon I was rewiring the workshop and the company offices, and then the company asked me to go on the road wiring apartment buildings and hospitals for television systems. This was the very beginnings of the cable industry, and I was to start working on what were called "master antenna" systems. In apartment buildings, for example, instead of each apartment having its own television antenna on the roof, all the apartments would be connected by coaxial cable to one television tower. Amplifiers were mounted on the tower and inside the building. I was very interested in the new job, but to do it, I would need a car.

The company was willing to compensate me for the use of the car, but I would have to buy it myself. I accepted the job and bought my first headache, I mean car! I bought a Morris Oxford, an import that gave me nothing but trouble. I learned the hard way that you get what you pay for. Fortunately, in 1954, I was able to buy my first brand-new car, a four-door Ford Mainline. I had some trouble getting used to driving it, though compared to my Morris, driving the Ford was like driving a very roomy tank.

I continued to make progress in the company, and soon I became a troubleshooter, installing and testing the amplifiers and other equipment needed to operate the cable systems in apartment buildings and hospitals. My salary now was $1.25 per hour. I was really coming up in the world!

After six years of working for the Toronto Television Company, I was ready to start out on my own. I was told that my salary, which had increased to $1.75 per hour, was the maximum I could earn. I set up my own company, Master Electronic Service, repairing televisions and troubleshooting apartment-building master systems. I began to get additional work as a troubleshooter for other companies that wired apartment buildings and hospitals. When the Princess Margaret Hospital expanded, because I had built their first installation in 1957 when I still worked for Toronto Television, they asked me to do all their electronics work, installing everything for their televisions and their paging and Muzak systems.

The hospital later gave me my own workshop in the building, and I provided electronic services to them for about twenty-five years, until I retired.

In January 1959, I started proceedings to officially adopt Katy and Philip, at their request. We had discussed the issue of adoption before, but my feeling had always been that if this was something the children wanted, they would ask for it when they were ready. And this is exactly what happened. Katy and Philip did not feel comfortable at school having the last name Pels when their parents both had the name Englishman. They asked if we could change this, and I told them what was involved. They decided that they were ready to go ahead. The official adoption papers came through on February 8, 1960, when Katy was twenty-one and Philip was eighteen.

While I was still at Toronto Television, a co-worker, William Binewych, and I had gotten to know each other very well. Bill was a top-notch electronics technician who mainly did bench work in the workshop on equipment that had to be sent in for repairs by technicians on the road. He decided to leave Toronto Television about the same time that I did, and he opened a store selling and repairing radios, televisions, and other electronic equipment. Because I knew how reliable he was, I started bringing my bench repair work to Bill's shop so that I would be free to provide road service. After a while, Bill asked me if I was interested in establishing a partnership. I accepted, and we became partners in a shop on Queen Street West. We made an unlikely team, a Ukrainian and a Jew. But as far as Bill and I were concerned, it was never a problem.

CHAPTER TEN

Déjà Vu

BECAUSE OUR STORE SPECIALIZED IN THE REPAIR OF TELEVISIONS, RADIOS, tape recorders, and so on, Bill and I were often visited by police detectives who were looking for stolen goods. One morning in the spring of 1963, five years after Bill and I had started our business together, a man whom I took to be a detective walked into the store and asked to speak to me in private. We went to the restaurant next door for a cup of coffee. He told me that he wasn't with the police force, although he had served with the Canadian Armed Forces intelligence service during the war. He knew all about the horrors of the concentration camps and that I was a Holocaust survivor. He never did tell me how he knew about any of this and, to this day, I'm still not sure how he happened to come to me. In any event, this man—I'll call him Irv—asked if I knew that a neo-Nazi party had been started in Toronto. My jaw dropped in surprise; I could not believe what I was hearing. Irv said that if I wanted proof, he would take me to the place where they held their meetings.

Later that night we met at the corner of Yonge Street and Davenport Road in downtown Toronto. He pointed out a building and the two of us watched as people arrived to attend a meeting that was being held on the main floor of a converted store. One of the emergency exit doors had been left partially open, in case a fast exit was needed. Irv and I stood there eating doughnuts and drinking coffee, listening to a speaker who clearly modelled himself in looks, mannerisms, and speech after Adolf Hitler. Watching him, I felt as though I had gone back in time and that the events of 1933 Germany were happening all over again.

I was so stunned that, for a while, I did not know what to say. But we had to do something. Irv and I decided that we should keep listening in on their meetings so that we could find out what was going on. We also took down the licence-plate numbers of everyone who came to the meetings. The so-called leaders and speakers were clever, though. They usually arrived in rented cars. The speeches were the usual ranting of Nazi propaganda—ravings about Jewish bankers, Jewish-owned newspapers, Jewish landlords, unreliable and untrustworthy Jewish businessmen, and, naturally, about a Jewish world conspiracy. These were the same words that had brought Hitler to power, only this time the main actors were John Beattie, who called himself head of the Canadian Nazi Party, and David Stanley.

As we eavesdropped on the meetings, we overheard the group planning a march in Nazi uniforms that was to be held in a downtown Toronto park known as Allan Gardens. A few days later, Irv called to tell me that swastika armbands and flags had arrived at the post office, and that the neo-Nazis had set a date for the march. I still have no idea how Irv got his information, but the news both alarmed and infuriated me. I told Irv that we needed help and that I wanted to let the Canadian Jewish Congress know what was going on. "Go right ahead," he said, "and see if you can get them to do anything."

I went to the congress and spoke to two leading members of the executive. They told me that the congress knew all about the march, and so I asked them what they were planning to do about it. They replied that the position of the executive was to do nothing, and that it would be much better if I also kept quiet. They explained that there were two reasons why I shouldn't make any kind of fuss about the neo-Nazis. The first reason was that they did not want to worry the Jewish people. The second was that they did not want to give the neo-Nazis any kind of publicity. I was flabbergasted. "You people haven't learned a thing from the Holocaust," I told them. "What you are doing is exactly what allowed the Nazis to seize power in Germany. From 1930 to 1945, the Dutch Jewish Congress played the same tune that I am hearing now. Many Jewish lives could have been saved if the Jewish people had been told the truth."

I knew that after all I had been through, I could not keep quiet. I told Irv that I was going to speak to all the different Jewish organizations and *landsmanshaften* (mutual benefit societies for Jewish immigrants from the same region in their former homelands), synagogues, and schools. He wished me luck, but said that it wasn't really his way of doing things. He was more interested in a direct, militant way of fighting this poison. I warned him that the two of us would not get very far without the co-operation of other Jewish groups.

One of the first people I spoke to was Jacob Egit, the executive director of the Histadrut, a Toronto organization named after the Labour Zionist Party in Israel. They conducted almost all their meetings in Yiddish, and their membership was quite large. When I explained what I knew and how I had obtained the information, Jacob Egit agreed to let me speak at their next general meeting. I was the only non-Yiddish-speaking person ever to address any of their meetings. As soon as they heard what I had to say, they promised to back me up all the way. I went on to approach the Young Men's Group of the Pride of Israel Synagogue, Harvey Lister of the Jewish Veterans, Sam Pasternak of the General Wingate branch of the Jewish Veterans, and Mike Burwald of N-3, a militant activist Jewish group that had formed in response to neo-Nazi anti-Semitism.

Over a period of time, I spoke to a great many people in all kinds of grassroots organizations, and every one of them agreed that something had to be done about the neo-Nazi march. I told them that the date for the march in Allan Gardens had been set for Sunday, May 30, 1965, and the Jewish groups all agreed to hold a counter-demonstration for the same day.

On the day of the rally, we gathered in Allan Gardens behind a police line that had been set up to try to keep the two groups apart. I watched from a side street as the neo-Nazis assembled in a line ready to march into the park. John Beattie, the leader of the Canadian Nazi party, walked in front carrying a swastika flag, followed by about thirty-five of his gang. Some of them were wearing swastika armbands. As soon as they stepped into the park at the corner of Carlton and Sherbourne streets, the counter-demonstrators surged forward, breaking through the police line. That is when half of the neo-Nazi group ran off and disappeared. The police were trying to prevent a riot, but they could not stop such a mass of people. The newspaper estimated that there were more than six thousand counter-demonstrators in Allan Gardens that day, and included in this number were a great many Holocaust survivors.

Emotions were running high, and this crowd was in no mood to let the neo-Nazis march in the park unopposed. The strength of the opposition proved to be too much for the fascists. As we came closer, the neo-Nazis began to run toward the nearest exit at Gerrard and Jarvis streets. The police moved in and started arresting some of our people, taking them to the nearest police station. Meyer Gasner, president of the Ontario Region of the Canadian Jewish Congress, went inside the police station and tried to get people released. I thought that I even caught a glimpse of certain members of the Canadian Jewish Congress, including some of their executive members, in the park as well. A lot has been written about what took place on that day in Allan Gardens, but one thing stands out in my mind: the very real pleasure of seeing the Nazis on the run instead of the Jews!

A few days after this incident, however, the Canadian Jewish Congress released a letter to the newspapers and to Toronto Jewish organizations in which they distanced themselves from the events in Allan Gardens. They went so far as to describe the counter-demonstrators as "uncivilized." The letter, signed by four members of the congress executive, outraged the Jewish community at large. Holocaust survivors contrasted the congress's comments with their own memories of thousands upon thousands of Jews marching in a "civilized" manner into the gas chambers. For the survivors, the Canadian Jewish Congress had lost all its credibility as leaders of the Jewish community. Some people questioned whether the congress represented the Jews or the Nazis. In a mass meeting of a number of Jewish organizations, people demanded that the congress remove the four executive members who had signed the letter. There was talk of disbanding the congress. I spoke out against the idea. I felt that we should not throw the baby out with the bathwater and that with democratically elected people on the executive, the congress could properly represent all members of the Jewish community.

A second mass meeting was held at Holy Blossom Temple, chaired by Rabbi Gunther Plaut. There, the Jewish community and the Canadian Jewish Congress came face to face. The congress executive promised that the congress would become a more democratically run organization and, as a result of that meeting, the Jewish community got much better representation.

No neo-Nazi group has ever again tried to hold the same kind of public demonstration in Toronto. In the fall of 1965, the neo-Nazis decided to hold a demonstration protesting a play that was being performed in a theatre on Bayview Avenue. The play was called *The Deputy,* by Rolf Hochhuth.

Apparently they did not like the play's interpretation of the Hitler Nazi period and they wanted to disrupt the performance. Again, Jews held a counter-demonstration and some of us, including me, were inside the theatre. We had a really good turnout because we were expecting the neo-Nazis to come inside and vandalize the theatre. But the police came out in force and warned the neo-Nazis that they could not guarantee their safety. The fascist group must have taken this warning seriously, because they turned back.

On January 29, 1967, we organized another large demonstration on Jarvis Street against CBC television for taping an interview with Adolf von Thadden, a German official who was well known for his war-time Nazi activities. This time the neo-Nazis announced a counter-demonstration, but when the police again warned that they could not protect them, these (brave) neo-Nazis changed their minds and did not show up.

Meanwhile, Irv and I continued to faithfully eavesdrop on the regular neo-Nazi meetings. We found out that a speaker from an extreme right-wing American group had been invited to address the Toronto group, and that the meeting was to be held in a hotel somewhere near Niagara Falls. Irv and I went there and spoke to the owner of the hotel, informing him about the people who had rented his space. We asked him to cancel the booking, but he was reluctant to do so. Then Irv, who looked like a plain-clothed police officer, told the owner that the police would not be able to protect him or his hotel from the damage that might occur during the meeting because the Jewish community in Toronto would be protesting the event. The hotel owner got the message and the meeting was cancelled.

So far we had succeeded in disrupting several neo-Nazi events, but now Irv and I started discussing how we might stop their regular meetings. We decided that the best way of doing so was to get our hands on their membership and mailing lists. Once we had these lists, we could let them know that we would publicize the names of all their members and supporters. We also found out that a number of neo-Nazis lived in a large house on Admiral Road. I decided to have a look inside the house to see what I could find out.

I put on my tool belt and took my field-strength meter with me. This particular instrument measured the power of an electromagnetic field. In this case it was actually designed to measure the strength of a television transmitter broadcasting from a TV station, but it looked very impressive.

I knocked on the door of the house and told the man who answered that I was an electrical troubleshooter working for the hydro company. I was trying to find the source of an electrical problem that we had traced to this house because of a very high meter reading. I asked if I could come inside to check it out and, if necessary, repair the problem. I looked so official that the man let me inside. I managed to get into every room in the house, and by pretending to do some work I made notes about all the windows and doors that let to the outside. I told the man that as far as I could tell, their installation looked all right to me, but if there was another unusual reading, I might have to come back. He said that was fine with him. As soon as I got outside, I drew the layout of the house, complete with all entrances and exits, in case I had to go back there.

One night when Irv and I were spying on another neo-Nazi meeting, we heard that they were planning a membership drive. All the regular members were told to bring prospective new members to the building during the day to register. I decided to become a registered member of the neo-Nazi party. I walked into the building but made sure that when I got to the desk there were other people ahead of me to occupy the man at the registration desk. I told him that I would wait for my turn, but in the meantime would it be all right with him if I looked around a bit? He told me to go right ahead.

I knew that beside the entrance to the neo-Nazi headquarters was another entrance at the back of the building, off Yonge Street, that led to a small hallway and stairs to the upper floors. I wanted to know if there was a door that led from the office where I was standing into that back entrance hall. I checked out a side door and found that, sure enough, it connected directly to the foyer of the second entrance. The door was bolted with several deadbolts. The neo-Nazis clearly were not taking any chances. I opened the deadbolts but left the regular lock that I knew I could easily open from the outside. Then I walked back to the man at the desk and told him that I had forgotten to pick something up and that I would be right back. Instead, I left.

I called Irv and told him that tonight was the night to go ahead with our plans to get into the building. I forgot to tell him that I had already been inside and prepared the way for us. When we met later that evening, Irv had brought some heavy-duty tools and a flashlight. I showed him the side door and he got ready to put his crowbar to work. Just as I stopped him a motorcycle policeman roared past. I loved the noise his motorcycle made because no one could hear me put my foot to the door. The door popped open and Irv stood there with his mouth open. I asked him to take his tools back to the car, but to keep his flashlight. Then we went inside, making sure not to make any noise because I had no idea if anyone was on the upper floors. Suddenly, while we were walking around the main floor of the building, Irv said, "Did you see that?" "See what?" I asked. "Watch the ceiling," he said. "Wherever I go, a light on the ceiling follows me." That gave me a really good laugh! Irv had put his flashlight in his back pocket with the lens facing up, but had forgotten to switch it off. We both felt much better after we had closed the curtain on the big window facing Yonge Street. I showed Irv the membership lists inside the desk and the metal trays with the card index. We removed the trays and the files, put them in our cars, and left. We did not touch anything else.

It turned out that we did not have to do anything at all with the names. The neo-Nazis called the police and the media and complained bitterly about the Jews who had stolen their membership and sponsor lists. The loss of their records put an end to their meetings and their other activities, because now everyone associated with them was too afraid that their names would be made public. It was a temporary victory, however, because although it was also the end of this particular group, other neo-Nazi groups sprang up later to take their place.

The groups that had participated in the earlier anti-Nazi events held more demonstrations, but now the Canadian Jewish Congress co-operated fully with us. We even met regularly in their offices.

One of the demonstrations we planned was held in front of the Inn on the Park Hotel, on Eglinton Avenue East in Toronto, in October 1971. Alexei Kosygin, then premier of the Soviet Union, was staying in the hotel in preparation for an address he was to give at the nearby Ontario Science Centre. Jewish organizations were coming out in full force to protest the Soviet policy that refused to allow Soviet Jews to emigrate.

As I have said, my business partner, Bill, was Ukrainian and he therefore had some connections to the Toronto Ukrainian community. Before Kosygin arrived in Toronto, Bill told me that he had learned that an anti-Soviet demonstration was being planned by a militant Ukrainian group. He warned me that the Jewish demonstrators should be kept away from the main entrance of the Inn on the Park. Bill and I had talked about

Kosygin's planned visit to Toronto, and he knew that I was deeply involved with the anti-neo-Nazi movement. He did not want the Jewish demonstration to be anywhere near the Ukrainian group because he was positive that something drastic was going to happen, and he did not want Jews to be blamed for it.

I took his warning seriously and brought it up at the next planning committee meeting at the Toronto Canadian Jewish Congress building. We were meeting to work out the details of the demonstration, and I asked that our demonstrators be kept on the south side of Eglinton Avenue, across from the Inn on the Park. I told the committee that there was a strong possibility that the actions of another group who were also planning a demonstration would result in violence. I did not name the group involved, but my proposal was accepted. It proved to be the right decision. A physical attack was made on Kosygin, and although security people prevented any serious injuries, the attacker was arrested. The media did not make a big issue of it and the Jews were not mentioned. I have often wondered how much publicity there would have been if the attacker had been a Jew.

Despite the success of our various actions against the neo-Nazis, as the years went by it became clear to me that trying to get legal action against Nazi war criminals or neo-Nazi activists was useless. I realized that if I wanted to stop the evil, I would have to find another way to fight.

CHAPTER ELEVEN

Fighting Back by Telling the Truth

SO MANY REQUESTS HAD BEEN MADE FOR A CENTRAL RESOURCE FOR HOLO-
caust education that in 1985 the United Jewish Appeal (UJA) Federation of
Greater Toronto set up the Holocaust Remembrance Committee and the
Holocaust Memorial Centre to educate students and other groups about
the history of the Holocaust.

When the program started, the Holocaust Remembrance Committee
asked survivors to come forward and tape their testimony as a permanent
record for others, especially young people, to learn about what happened
to the Jews in World War II. The committee also asked survivors if they were
willing to speak to students and other groups about their experiences. The
idea appealed to me as a way of reaching the younger generation and educating them about the Holocaust. I felt as though I had been wasting my
time chasing Nazis when it was clear that they were never going to be held
accountable for their crimes. The educational work that the Holocaust
Centre was doing promised to be much more rewarding.

I haven't been disappointed. Every year, twenty-five thousand students and other visitors come through the centre itself, and the outreach
program arranges for Holocaust survivors to speak in Toronto schools.
When a group first arrives at the centre, they are greeted by a docent, a
volunteer guide, who explains what people will see and hear as they go
through. The first exhibit is a thirty-minute slide show about the Holocaust
that was prepared and written by Paula Draper and narrated by Lorne
Green. It is an educational account of the persecution and murder of European Jews during World War II. Most of the photographs in the slide show

Michael speaking to students about the Holocaust

were taken by the German concentration camp guards and commanders, but some of the pictures were taken by the Allied liberation forces when they entered the camps. After the slide show is over, a Holocaust survivor takes over and speaks to the group about the experience of living under the Nazi regime as a Jew and about being in the camps. Of course, one of the most important aspects of the program is the question and answer session at the end.

I started with the program in April 1988, and since then I have spoken to all kinds of people at public schools, high schools, colleges, universities, synagogues, churches, special schools run by groups such as Amish and Mennonites, libraries, police forces, and, once, a large group of psychiatrists. My work at the centre has also turned out to be just the beginning. Every year I participate in Holocaust Education Week, which has been proclaimed annually by the mayor of Toronto in the first week of November since 1981. During that week, churches, libraries, bookstores, schools, synagogues, and renowned local, national, and international speakers all participate in various aspects of Holocaust studies. And for the last eight years, I have been invited to speak at the "Annual Student Seminar Day on the Holocaust" for teachers and students at the Ontario Institute for Studies in

Education. At the end of the seminar, I often hear from the teachers in the audience, "You did more in two hours than we can do in two years of Holocaust teaching."

Comments like these give survivors an incentive to go on with the work, even though it isn't easy to speak publicly about what we experienced and to be bombarded with questions. But I have learned that the more questions I am asked, the better the class. Now I start to worry when I don't get enough questions. Over the years that I have been speaking to groups about the Holocaust, many of the same questions have come up again and again. Here are some of the most commonly asked questions and the way that I usually answer them.

How could the Holocaust have happened in a democratic country like Germany?
As a fully democratic country, Germany adhered strictly to the principle of freedom of speech. I believe that Hitler took full advantage of this freedom and used his democratic rights to destroy democracy in Germany. He used the media of the time—radio and newspapers—to disseminate his hatred for Jews and other non-Aryans. He blamed the non-Aryans for Germany's economic and political problems and convinced the German people that by "suspending" democracy, he could bring Aryan Germans to their rightful place as a world power. This experience has taught me that freedom without any restrictions is as dangerous as a car without any brakes—the potential for destruction is enormous.

Why did Hitler pick on the Jews?
A minority is always an easy target and the Nazis needed a scapegoat for Germany's problems. Historically, Jews were often considered to be "outsiders."

Why didn't the Jews resist? Was there any type of resistance in the concentration camps?
Resistance inside the camps was extremely dangerous because anyone who stepped out of line would be shot on the spot—and not just this person alone; all the other prisoners in the same barracks would be punished as well. But it's a myth that Jews didn't resist at all. The Jews in the Warsaw ghetto in Poland were the only civilian group to stage an open, armed

revolt against the Nazis. The Jews fought them barehanded and with Molotov cocktails and stolen guns against German tanks and artillery. In April 1943 the Jews drove the Germans out of the ghetto, but in May the German troops destroyed the Jewish underground headquarters and the Jewish leader Mordechai Anielewicz. Fifty-six thousand Jews were killed or deported; fifteen thousand managed to escape. The uprising lasted three weeks—longer than the resistance mounted by the armed forces in many of the countries Hitler invaded.

In Amsterdam Jews staged an uprising that started in Waterlooplein Square, and the Dutch underground also managed to burn part of the registry building that housed the records of Dutch Jewish citizens. Even inside the camps, prisoners were able to find small ways to sabotage the Germans.

Many Jews managed to escape and form partisan groups in the forest. Homemade hand grenades and bombs were manufactured in secret workshops. A small supply of arms was purchased for exorbitant sums on the black market with some co-operation from the communists and the Polish underground.

The Warsaw ghetto uprising proved the myth of Nazi "invincibility" to be false. Although the Germans crushed the revolt, German prestige was very much undermined.

Why did only a handful of people help the Jews?
Many courageous individuals did help hide Jews, especially Jewish children, and saved them from certain death in the concentration camps. The penalty for helping Jews was severe. Those who did speak out against the Nazis paid with their lives.

What kind of food did you eat in the concentration camps?
Well, we never had to worry about too many calories! Most of the time we got a daily ration of thin soup made from cauliflower leaves and a small piece of hard, dry bread that was barely enough to feed a bird.

What were the worst experiences you had in the concentration camps?
There were many, but some of the worst experiences that I had in the camps were witnessing the decapitation of a prisoner right in front of my eyes in Birkenau and the brutal hangings in the Nordhausen section of concentration camp Dora.

Were you very happy when you were liberated?
No, I was not. I was sure that terrible things had happened to my family and that I was the sole survivor.

How did the Red Cross act during the war?
I think that the Red Cross behaved shamefully during the war by their lack of action. If they had forced the Nazis to consider Jews in the concentration camps to be prisoners of war, our conditions would have been very different. Prisoners in the camps called them "Hitler's Red Cross."

Who established that six million Jews died? How was that figure arrived at?
The figure of six million actually came from the Nazi administration. They kept very careful records of their death industry.

It was also the German guards who took the pictures of the mass graves and how they came to be; for instance, the Jews had to dig a large pit and then they were machine-gunned. Then other Jews had to fill up the hole with earth again.

There was also the *sunder commando,* Jews who were selected to work in the gas chambers, where they had to cut the hair off, remove the clothing, shoes, eyeglasses, luggage, and everything else that was useful to the Germans. The sunder commando also had to put the bodies into the crematorium and remove the ashes.

Shortly after we were liberated I was told that the sunder commando had revolted. Some of them had managed to escape in the forest, and the rest of them were killed.

After the liberation, what did you think about religion?
My view of religion was badly shaken. I thought, did G-d not see what was happening? Was G-d asleep? But after I had discussions with clergy from different faiths, I accepted their explanation that G-d does not control people. People control people. I also found that I missed the Jewish way of life that I had been used to before the war.

How can you recognize a war criminal after so many years?
I can only speak for myself, but I would recognize Mr. Ritter, for example, by his way of walking, his manner of speaking, his eyes, and his general behaviour. However, I would have to actually see him in order to recognize

him. The process of showing survivors pictures of men in their seventies in civilian clothes is very problematic. It is often impossible for us to identify them as the young men in uniform that we had known more than fifty years ago.

What are your feelings about the prosecution of war criminals?
I have mixed feelings about war criminal trials. Yes, the world should know who these people are and, yes, they should be called to account and punished for what they did. I don't understand why it took fifty years for many countries to realize the necessity of doing so. However, I believe that educating young people about the Holocaust is a far more effective way of ensuring that it never happens again.

What made you decide to speak out now after all these years?
Even now it is very hard to find the words to properly describe the horrors of the concentration camps. Please realize that all the camp survivors were Europeans whose native tongue is not English. For many years, I could not find the right words to describe my experiences in my own language—how could I do this in English?

Could there be another Holocaust?
Yes, a Holocaust could happen again. Just look at what has happened recently in the Balkans and what is happening right now in parts of Africa.

Could anything be done to prevent it?
The first thing that we can do to prevent another Holocaust is to speak out against racism and hatred. That is why I am devoting so much of my time to speaking to students. You can make a difference. You may think that you don't need to worry about this now, but you must remember that no one took the Nazis seriously in the beginning. In 1930 everyone thought they were a joke. By 1945, no one was laughing.

Have you ever been sorry that you are a Jew?
No, it has never entered my mind to regret being Jewish. The problem is not with my being a Jew, but with the racism that leads some people to hate others enough to commit acts of unspeakable violence.

What are your people doing about today's neo-Nazis?
Neo-Nazis are not just a Jewish problem. Racism and hatred is something
that everybody must fight. I consider it my duty to fight the neo-Nazi
denial of the Holocaust by doing what I am doing right now—telling the
truth about what happened. As long as the courts are unable to stop the
Holocaust deniers, we, the survivors, must do the job through education.
After all, we are the only ones who know the truth.

The questions I am asked when I am teaching at the Holocaust Centre
show how little most students really know about what happened in World
War II. The more I do this work, the more I realize how much it needs to
be done. For the most part, the students are eager to learn, but, of course,
there are occasionally a few neo-Nazi skinheads in the audience. These
students usually do what they do best: when they are challenged head on,
they either hide or run. One student was extremely disruptive; however,
he was not a neo-Nazi but a young Palestinian man. Before I start speaking to a group, I usually ask the students to save their questions until the
end. During my presentation, however, this young man insisted on con-
tinually interrupting me. When I finally asked him why he was doing this,
he stood up and said, "I'm a Muslim." I asked him if that was a problem;
there were students from several different religions and ethnic cultures in
the class. He said that he was trying to make a point: "I want to tell the students here that the Israeli troops who occupy our territory are the Nazis
of the Middle East."

I stopped him right there. I explained to the class that I was not here
to discuss politics. Other people were much more qualified for this than
I. "But," I told the student, "since you have made your statement to the
class, would you now be so kind as to tell us whether you've ever lived in
a country that was occupied by the Nazis." Of course, his answer was no.
I said, "I have lived in a country that was occupied by the Nazis, so I'll tell
you what would have happened if one of us had thrown stones at a German soldier the way that Palestinians throw stones at Israeli soldiers. Not
only would the person who threw the stone be shot on the spot, but anyone who was standing anywhere in the vicinity would also have been shot
because, unlike the Israelis, the German soldiers didn't use rubber bullets.
Israeli soldiers might demolish a house looking for terrorists, but first they
clear out the occupants; German soldiers put people into a house before

burning it, and shot anyone trying to escape. I think that I've made my point," I continued. "Would you now please sit down so that I can continue or would you prefer to leave?" He sat down and there were no further disruptions.

In addition to my work at the Holocaust Centre, I have also continued to be active in various community organizations. I joined the Pride of Israel Sick Benefit Society and Synagogue in 1960, and was almost immediately elected to the executive. When we moved to the Pride of Israel's new synagogue building on Bathurst Street in 1967, I became a member of the board of governors. In 1971 I was elected house chairman of the Pride of Israel. I was supposed to hold the position for two years, but almost thirty years later, guess who is still house chairman? In 1983 and 1984 I was honoured to be elected chairman of the synagogue at the same time that my wife Rika was elected chairwoman of the Sisterhood, the women's auxiliary of the Pride of Israel synagogue.

I also love to sing and joined the professional choir of the Shaarei Shomayim Synagogue in 1966, which was trained and conducted by the late Cantor Nathan Adler. While I was in the choir, I became very good friends with Morris Goldlust and his family. We often travelled together on holidays, to Israel, to Italy, and even to Holland. But on that first trip back to Holland in March 1973, I couldn't stay longer than three days. I still found it too painful because I had not given up searching for my family, all to no avail.

In September 2000, the government of Canada conducted a ceremony to recognize and thank survivors of the Holocaust. I was able to attend the presentation, as these pictures illustrate.

Michael with great-grandson Cole at the September 2000 event
recognizing the work of Holocaust survivors

Michael, with his certificate from the Government of Canada, is congratulated by
Joel Dmitry, chair of the Canadian Society for Yad Vashem (left) and
Deputy Prime Minister Herb Gray.

Copy of the certificate presented to Michael on the fifty-fifth anniversary of the liberation from the camps

CHAPTER TWELVE

Family Reunion

IN THE WINTER OF 1994, MY SON PHILIP MET A DUTCH GIRL IN FLORIDA AND later in the year decided to travel to Holland to visit her. While he was in Holland, he happened to pick up a telephone directory, and to his amazement he found a listing for Engelschman, spelled the same way we spell our name in Dutch. Philip decided to make a telephone call, and sure enough he was put in touch with an uncle of the person he called.

Right away Philip called me from Holland and told me that he had found some of our family. I thought that he was either joking or that he'd been drinking. But Philip insisted that he had talked to Louis Engelschman, whose father and my father were brothers. He said that Louis had shown Philip proof that we were related and gave me Louis's telephone number. I called as soon as I got off the phone with Philip and had a long conversation with my new-found first cousin, Louis. He explained that I had never known about that part of my father's family because my father's brother, Louis's father, had married out of the faith before I was born. My family was Orthodox, and intermarriage was forbidden. Most of the Engelschman family had sat shiva for Louis's father; that is, they had declared him dead. To them he was. Although I had never known my father to be a fanatic, I don't remember anyone in my family ever talking about any of this.

I was also surprised to hear from my new-found cousin that my father had supplied their family with matzo, which is the unleavened bread that is eaten during Passover. These matzos were packed in large, round boxes and were picked up at our house by the oldest brother, Henry. This proves that my father and his family were keeping in touch with each other without any of us children knowing about it.

When I had returned to Amsterdam from the concentration camps, there were no telephone directories to look people up and, because the registration office had listed my family as having died in the camps, Louis's side of the family had given up looking for survivors. As far as I knew, just one person who had survived the war held the key to both sides of our family: my cousin Duifje. I knew that she had survived because she had actually come to my house in Amsterdam after I returned from the camps. Unfortunately, I never got a chance to speak to her. My eyes were very bad then, and by the time I got downstairs, she had disappeared. I had no idea what her married name was, and I had no way of finding her.

It turns out, though, that Louis had been working on a family tree for the past ten years and had learned that I was living in Toronto. Several years before, on a trip to the United States, he had come up to Toronto to find me. He had looked me up in the Toronto telephone directory but could not find my name because he was looking for Michel Engelschman. He had no way of knowing that I now spelled my name the English way, Englishman. After that last attempt, Louis had given up trying to find me.

But now that we had spoken, Louis couldn't wait to have a family reunion, and he planned one for September 1994. Unfortunately, in August of that year, I had a heart attack and needed coronary bypass surgery. Needless to say, I was in no shape to travel. As soon as I recovered, though, we rescheduled the reunion, and Rika, Katy, her husband Danny, Philip, and I arrived in Holland on Friday, May 12, 1995. We were greeted at the airport by Louis Engelschman and Rika's cousin, Elizabeth Van Buiten, her husband, Jan, and their son, Benny.

When I first arrived in Amsterdam, I was forced to rest for a few days while my foot recovered from an infection. But as soon as I was able to get around, my son-in-law, Danny, went with me to my former house on the Plantage Muidergracht. I wanted to try once more to get inside the house and look for the papers I had left there. I rang the doorbell and this time, when I explained who I was and that I was looking for pictures of my family that had been hidden inside a wall during the war, the man who lived there invited me to come upstairs. Once I was inside the fourth-floor apartment, I could see right away that the place had been completely renovated. The wall where the pictures had been hidden had been removed and just the outside brick wall remained. I was out of luck. The man took a very old Dutch New Testament Bible off a shelf and told me that he had found it inside the ceiling of the middle room where we were standing. He didn't have the heart to throw it out, he said. "I always had the feeling that someone would show up to claim this Bible. Now that you're here, I'll hand it over to you to do with as you please." I took it reluctantly because I was sure that it had not belonged to my family; I couldn't imagine why my father would have hidden a Bible inside our ceiling. But I thanked the man for his kind thoughts and took the Bible with me. I saved it and brought it back to Canada.

I was deeply disappointed to realize once and for all that my family pictures were gone forever, but I had made my decision forty years before to look forward, not back. I devoted the rest of my time to enjoying some of the sights in and around Amsterdam with my family.

The night before the family reunion, another of my new-found cousins, Louis's brother, Ruud, and his wife, Rita, invited us for dinner at their house because they were not going to be able to attend the next day's events. Their children and grandchildren were there as well. When Ruud and I were sitting beside each other, the family resemblance was so strong that my son-in-law, Danny, couldn't resist taking a picture of us. Even I could see how much we looked alike. It shouldn't have surprised me so much; we are, after all, first cousins. But after all those years of thinking that I had no family, it was truly amazing.

A family reunion of about forty members of the Engelschman clan was held on May 21, 1995, in a hotel in Bunnik, near the city of Utrecht. It was wonderful. Not only had I not met most of these people, I didn't know they existed! During the festivities, Louis presented me with a heavy roll of wallpaper. On the back of it, he had laid out our family tree. He had been able to trace our family back to 1780. I was overwhelmed by the amount of work he had done.

At the party I met all kinds of cousins: my first cousins Hennie, Walter, and Louis, who were brothers; another first cousin, Barend; and the rest of their families. While I was talking to Barend, I suddenly realized that the woman who had come to my house in Amsterdam after the war, and then disappeared without seeing me, was Barend's sister, my cousin Duifje. When she had come to my house all those years ago, I didn't know who she was; my eyes were so bad then that I literally couldn't see her. She, of course, knew nothing about my eye condition and may have thought that I did not want to see her. But I'll never know exactly what happened. Duifje was not able to attend the reunion because she was (and still is) living in an old-age home and suffering from Alzheimer's disease.

Barend told me that I might be able to meet with Duifje, who had decided that she now wanted to be called Deena. He would make arrangements with the old-age home to pick her up and take her to his house for the day. Louis was also very interested in meeting her because he hoped that she would be able to fill in some information about the family. We set a date to meet for lunch at Barend's home in the town of Mijdrecht. Louis and I got there before noon on the appointed day, and there we met Deena. What followed was like a scene from a comedy show. Deena refused to talk to me because, according to her, I was not Michel Engelschman. In Deena's state of mind, she remembered me as I was before the war. She made every attempt to prove that she was right by asking me, through Barend, all kinds of trick questions about my family. We had come to try to get information about the family from her, but she had turned the tables and managed to get information from us! However, some of the things that Deena said that day proved to me that she was the person who had come to my home after the war. She was the only person in my family who was in Amsterdam after the war, and she remembered very specific details about my family that no one else would know about. Unfortunately I never was able to convince her that I was Michel. In fact, during the whole encounter, she turned her back to me and spoke through Louis; she never spoke to me directly.

A few days later, Louis and his friend Jeanne invited us for a tour in the city of Rotterdam. This was the first city in Holland to be bombarded by a great number of German airplanes during the invasion of Holland. They wiped out the whole centre core of the city. Twenty years later, the city had been totally rebuilt.

After the reunion and my visit with Deena, we spent our last few days in Holland enjoying lazy visits with friends and members of our extended family. Rika, Katy, Danny, Philip, and I all went together to visit Ennie Jansen, Anna Mandic's niece, who had helped look after Katy and Philip during the war, and her husband Johan, in Limburg.

A funny thing happened while we were in Limburg. Danny and I were standing in front of a watch store when Danny's watchband broke. I suggested that we take the watch inside the store to have a new band put on. When we came back an hour later to pick up the watch, the owner of the store heard us talking and asked where Danny was from. When I said "Canada," he refused to take any money for the new watchband, saying, "I won't take money from a Canadian. It is my way of saying thank you." The Dutch people never forgot that it was Canadian troops who had liberated Holland from the Nazis in 1945.

Our visit was drawing to a close, and on one of our last days in Amsterdam, we went to the Albert Cuyp Straat to visit the open street market. After that, Rika and I went to the Sephardic cemetery in the town of Ouderkerk to visit the gravesite of Rika's mother, who had been buried there in 1935. We didn't know of any other member of either of our families who would have a grave in Holland because everyone else had died in the concentration camps. When Rika and I returned to Amsterdam from the camps, and when we returned to Holland from Canada the first time, we made a point of going to the grave to say Kaddish, the Jewish mourning prayer for the dead. But this time while we were at the cemetery, something unexpected happened. This time I had trouble finding Rika's mother's gravestone. The cemetery is over four hundred years old and it was very hard to read the names on the stones. I thought I knew where the stone was supposed to be, but I couldn't find it. I walked up and down the narrow paths between the stones, with no luck. Rika couldn't walk any further, so I found a bench for her to sit on and continued my search in a different part of the cemetery. Suddenly I realized that I had just passed a brand-new gravestone.

It was odd to see a new stone in this section of the cemetery, so I backed up to read the names that were engraved on the marble. As I read the names Ereira and Engelschman, I could feel my skin crawl and the hairs on the back of my neck stand on end. The names were spelled correctly; there was no mistake. This stone had been put there for two families: my own family and another family I had known very well, the Ereira family. My father's sister, Sara, was married to Philip Ereira, whom my mother affectionately called "Flip-Jan." The stone had been put there in memory of all the members of the two families who had no graves because they died in the concentration camps.

I went straight to the groundskeeper's house and asked her if she could tell me how this stone had come to be there. The woman couldn't

*Gravestone of Michael's aunt and uncle in an old
Sephardic cemetery, visited in May 1995*

remember offhand the name of the person who had paid for the stone. All
she knew was that she was a granddaughter of the person who was buried
there. The groundskeeper said that she would need more time to go through
the files to find the name because the stone had been put there the year
before. In the meantime, she showed us where Rika's mother's gravestone
was. Like many of the other gravestones in the old cemetery that had gone
unrepaired for so long, the writing on the stone had become unreadable.
That's why I had had so much trouble finding it.

I didn't have time to wait for the groundskeeper to look up the information on the new stone I had found because we were booked on a flight
back to Canada the next day. I asked Louis if he had come across this
granddaughter when he was constructing the family tree, but he didn't
have any idea who she might be. He promised to follow up with the
groundskeeper. We had time for one last visit before we left Holland, so Rika

and I spent some time with Ado and Melly Broodboom. We shared lunch, and a lot of nostalgia.

Five days later, when I was back in Canada, my phone rang at five o'clock in the morning. In his enthusiasm, Louis had forgotten all about the six-hour time difference between Amsterdam and Toronto. He was very excited because he had found our first cousin Margaret. Margaret Van Schaik-Ereira's mother was Sara Engelschman, my father's sister. Before the war, Margaret and I had been very close. I used to call her Greetje, which is short for Margaret, because she was quite short; she was probably only five feet (152 centimetres) on her tiptoes. Louis gave me her telephone number and I called her. Our conversation was very emotional, and she promised to visit us.

The following January, Margaret came to see us in Florida. Rika and I were waiting for her about two hundred feet (sixty metres) from the customs exit at the Miami airport. I recognized her as soon as I caught a glimpse of her and I called out, "Greetje!" She dropped whatever she was carrying and shouted, "Mickey!" I practically lifted her off the floor. She stayed with us for three weeks. It was as if a whole new world had opened up for us. Here was someone who had been very close to my family, someone whom I remembered very well, a very lovely person.

Since then, Greetje has come twice to visit us in Toronto. In July 1996, she stayed with us for another three weeks. It was such a pleasure to have her here with us; our children, grandchildren, and great-grandchildren are simply in love with her. And in October 1997, Greetje came to Canada again to celebrate the High Holidays with us.

I don't think that I will ever forget that trip to Holland, it gave me back family that I thought I had lost forever.

Would this ease the pain, the everlasting pain? No, nothing ever will.

No living soul should have to endure what my eyes have seen. But I will not give Hitler a posthumous victory. There is still an open sore inside of me that will never heal!

My wife and I started a new family from the ashes of the Holocaust. Was it easy? No. Did it pay? You bet it did! To be able to survive all the horrific experiences, and then, with my wife, to be able to show off children, grandchildren, and great-grandchildren could be considered a miracle.

CHAPTER THIRTEEN

March of the Living—April 2004

THE MARCH OF THE LIVING IS AN ANNUAL MARCH BETWEEN THE CONCEN-tration camps Auschwitz and Birkenau in Poland to commemorate the enormous slaughter of people that took place in all the concentration camps during World War II. This annual event is supported by the United Jewish Appeal (UJA). The M.O.L. starts in Poland and after one week there, all participants traveled to Israel for another week to participate in their programs.

Our group consisted of approximately 120 students plus several staff members, chaperones (including me), two doctors, two rabbis, and a video-grapher. We left Toronto on Wednesday, April 14, 2004.

We arrived the next day in Warsaw, Poland, and met with groups from all over the world, including clergy of different faiths.

When we arrived in Warsaw, our tour buses were waiting ready to take us to Gensha, Europe's largest Jewish cemetery. Then they took us back again to Warsaw, "The City of Monuments," and into the Warsaw Ghetto. Four hundred thousand Jewish people lived in this district. Some of the old walls are still standing. It was in the Warsaw Ghetto that the Jews started an armed open revolt against the Nazis that lasted three weeks. This was in April 1943. The Warsaw Ghetto uprising was the first open, organized revolt in all of Nazi-occupied Europe.

I had two self-proclaimed body guards, Dr. Isser Dubinsky, my room-mate for the trip, and Zack Belzberg. Dear Lord, please tell me, what did I do to deserve Zack? At seventeen years old, he was a heck of a nice young man.

What follows is my diary from that memorable trip.

Friday, April, 16, 2004

4:30 a.m. wake-up call. Breakfast and on to the bus to concentration camp Treblinka, which was a three-hour drive from Warsaw. On the way we stopped in Tykocin, a small village that has a mass grave in the forest solely of Jewish bodies from the concentration camps. This grave reminded me that I was supposed to be in there also!

This was the first time in sixty-four years that I cried. I firmly believed that I could never cry, but this one threw me for a loop because it reminded me of the time when we had to evacuate the concentration camp Buna and started our "Death March."

Back on to the bus to concentration camp Treblinka. We entered an wide open space with 1,600 upright slabs of rock, signifying the cities, towns, and villages from which the Jews were taken to their death. We saw the floor of the crematorium, which is all that was left. All of the barracks had been destroyed. The bus took us back to Warsaw.

Saturday April, 17, 2004

I slept for seven hours straight—a record for me since 1940. After breakfast, my roommate Isser and I attended a religious service inside our hotel, which was led by Rabbi Lori Cohen.

We actually had more of a discussion between us than a religious service, and touched on different subjects. Rabbi Lori led the discussions. This program was very well received by everyone. Our group of students, in general, were really bright.

Later on, we walked through Warsaw to the Jewish Ghetto and then back to our hotel for a special program. Seymour Epstein, a specialist on education and one of our staff, spoke on the subject of general education. Anita Ekstein, one of the chaperones, and I both spoke on the subject of the "Hidden Children." These were children hidden by non-Jews, often in the countryside by farmers—during the war. Shortly after, our staff was called for a meeting. We went to sleep at one a.m.

Sunday, April 18, 2004

Wake-up call at 6.15 a.m. At 7:00 a.m. onto the bus to Krakow, arriving at approximately 11:00 a.m. In Krakow we walked into what was once the Jewish district. We also drove by Oskar Schindler's factory, where he saved 1,200 Jewish people during the war.

Back onto the bus to concentration camp Treblinka, arriving about 8:00 p.m., at which time we checked into our hotel.

At 10:00 pm. we held a special memorial service in our hotel. I was asked to speak. This was just the right place to elaborate on the "Death March" in 1944.

Monday, April 19, 2004

This was the day of the memorial service. The bus took us to concentration camp Auschwitz. On the bus we were handed a wooden marker on which to write all the names of our immediate family who perished in the concentration camps.

We arrived in Auschwitz at 9:45 a.m., where we assembled with other groups and lined up, seven thousand of us in rows of eight, and started our walk to Birkenau in total silence. It was a walk of approximately four kilometres.

The security was enormous, with police and army personnel blocking the roads and streets. Fire trucks were stationed inside the concentration camp. There were dignitaries and representatives of governments all over the world as well as clergy of different faiths who addressed this crowd of about ten thousand people from all over the world, including a great number of Israelis.

It felt very strange to walk into this concentration camp with a camera in my hand.

Our Canadian students' choir was joined by students from Australia and New Zealand. Cantor Adler from Poland, who has a very beautiful voice, sang a special memorial prayer.

The outdoor stage was so large that a tractor-trailer could make a U-turn on it. It was on this stage that I said the Kaddish (a prayer for the deceased) to the assembly, and when I finished, I felt that I had completed a duty long overdue.

After the ceremony, our group went to one of the barracks for a special service. Back in our hotel at 10:30 p.m., where our staff had a short meeting, and then to sleep.

Tuesday, April, 20, 2004

5:30 a.m. wake-up call. Loaded our luggage into the bus and on our way to different places. While on the bus, Isser spoke to our group about unexplainable things that have happened to some of his patients who, against all the predictions, stayed alive until a certain person or thing appeared, then they let go of life.

Then it was my turn to take the microphone. I spoke about an article I had written several years ago, named "Was There a Guiding Hand?" I described several things that had happened to me without having a logical explanation, including the reunion with my family that began with Philip's discovery of the family name in the telephone directory, as described in the previous chapter. This talk was very well received.

We were now on the road to the Carpathian Mountains. In one of the towns we passed through, there was the remnant of a thousand-year-old synagogue. We had dinner at our hotel in Tarnów and at 9:45 p.m. we started a special program in the banquet hall. Everyone was seated against the walls on chairs or on the floor. A candle was lit and all the lights were switched off. The candle was passed from one person to the next. Each person holding the candle was to report, in short, how the experiences from the past week had affected him or her. When it was my turn to report, I stated that, during the ceremony in Birkenau, I watched from the stage and saw about ten thousand very dedicated people, Jews, non-Jews, dignitaries, clergy, young and old. They were the proof that Hitler, even after killing millions of Jews, had still lost his war against the Jews.

Wednesday, April 21, 2004
Wake-up call at 6:00 a.m. Packed and had breakfast. There was no such thing as a breakfast without very hard boiled eggs. As a matter of fact, if you happened to drop a peeled egg on the floor, it would bounce right back onto your plate!

We took our luggage to the bus for a trip to the eastern border of Poland and to the concentration camp Majdanek. A large structure had been built in the centre of the concentration camp, with a dome resting on pillars that stand on a 10 metre tall concrete wall. Inside the memorial is a mountain of human ashes, which we could see from a walkway around the top of the wall. As we walked we were shocked by what we saw. We climbed the steps to the walkway and as we looked at the ashes parts of human bones were visible, including a child's hip bone. Our rabbis conducted a special service right there.

Back onto the buses on our way to Warsaw and then to the airport for our flight to Israel with LOT Airlines.

Thursday, April 22, 2004

Israel, here we come!! We were on our way there to observe Israel's Memorial Day and to celebrate Israel's Independence Day.

At 12:30 a.m. dinner was served on the airplane. Some students from our group actually ate everything that was served!

We arrived in Tel Aviv at 3:00 a.m. and got on the bus around 4:30 a.m., entering Jerusalem by 6:00 a.m. right at the Western Wall, which was full of bullet holes from the last war. People from different countries were there for prayer.

After prayer we had breakfast and then proceeded by bus to the Dead Sea Spa in Ein Gedi for some relaxation.

At 4:00 p.m. we boarded the buses back to Jerusalem to a location with Bedouin hospitality. We entered a large tent where dinner was being served. We sat on the floor, no tables, no chairs, no cutlery, just finger-licking good! After dinner there was a demonstration of hand drums, large and small. Then the Bedouins started to sing while playing their drums. Lots of noise, but not unpleasant. At 10:00 p.m. we went back to our hotel.

Friday, April 23, 2004

4:00 a.m. Wake-up call for the students because they were going to Masada. They would be making the long and strenuous climb to the top of Masada. 6:00 a.m. wake-up call for the remaining elderly chaperones, who would be taking the cable car up to the top instead of walking. We arrived at Masada by 8:00 a.m. and had breakfast with the students. When we returned to Jerusalem we were given twenty minutes for lunch and shopping and then we went to a kibbutz with a guest house, Neve Ilan, for Sabbath dinner.

Saturday, April 24, 2004

Up at 7:30 a.m. I was the only one for breakfast in the dining room, large enough to seat three hundred people—no lineup!

We attended a Sabbath service led by Rabbi Lori Cohen. After lunch Isser asked me to go for a walk. We went to a lookout point from which we had an unbelievable view of the Old City of Jerusalem and its valleys.

At 5:00 p.m. Adina Katz, our videographer asked me for an interview, which lasted well over two hours.

At 9:00 p.m. we were back on the bus to Kibbutz Ramat Rachel, where we went into a large hall to find disco dancing with the volume control wide open and three hundred students screaming at the top of their lungs. Isser and I managed to escape to an outside lounge.

Sunday, April 25, 2004

At 12:30 a.m. we went back to our hotel, packed, and then went to bed. Wake-up call 6:15 a.m. Breakfast, and on our way to Yad Vashem, a monument to commemorate the people who died during the Nazi Holocaust. The floors of Yad Vashem are inscribed with the names of the most notorious extermination camps. In the Valley of the Communities, the names of all the communities that had citizens who perished in the concentration camps were carved in stone.

We then travelled to Ammunition Hill, in East Jerusalem, where an important battle of the Six Day War was fought. We walked inside the trenches and watched an excellent film about the Six Day War.

At 6:00 p.m. we arrived at a kibbutz in Tiberias near the Sea of Galilee.

At 9:30 p.m. I spoke to my own group of students, answering their questions, and then I went off to sleep.

Monday, April 26, 2004

6:15 a.m. wake-up call. Breakfast in a kibbutz could last you for the rest of the day; that means very much and very good. After breakfast we drove to Tzefat, which has a beautiful panoramic view of the surrounding landscape.

Today is Yom Hazikaron (Remembrance Day). At 11:00 a.m. the sirens started all over the country. All traffic stops for two minutes. Passengers and drivers get out of their vehicles and everyone stands at attention in total silence.

Back onto the bus on our way to Mount Meron, which is the highest mountain in Israel. We had our lunch on the top of the mountain. From there we travelled to Latrun. The scenery was just beautiful. We saw many sheepherders with lots of goats. We watched a film about the Six Day War at the Latrun Armoured Corpse Museum and then attended an outdoor stage service with a choir. Two thousand chairs were set up for us, but a number of people were still standing.

At 7:00 p.m. the celebrations of Independence Day started. There was singing where our choir was joined by an Australian choir, and from there we went to Mini Israel, a theme park that provided an outdoor location for a big party. Isser and I went back to our hotel because he was not feeling well. I told him to take two aspirins and call me in the morning, which he did, at 4:00 a.m.! After our conversation we went back to sleep.

Tuesday, April 27, 2004

After breakfast the bus took us to an air force base to watch a special air show, arriving at 11:30 a.m. Because we were the March of the Living Group, they allowed us on the base to watch the air show, but we were not to use our cameras. After going through the metal detector we all were stamped on the back of our hand. The woman soldier who stamped our hands saw the concentration camp number on my arm. She squeezed my hand and said, "There, now you have an extra number. Good luck."

The air show was spectacular, and the equipment unbelievable. We then drove to Herzliya and its beach on the Mediterranean Sea.

At 3:00 p.m. I had a camera interview with one of the students. From there we drove to the Chavat-Ronit arena. Enormous! There were approximately five thousand students from all over the world having dinner sitting at tables outdoors. We served ourselves from all kinds of different foods spread out over large tables. We watched dance groups from different nationalities. Students danced to disco music, mixing together like one big family. At 10:00 p.m. the fireworks started—what a show! We went back to our hotel in Tel Aviv to try to sleep, but no way. The students were noisy, excited, and over tired. We were leaving tonight for home.

Wednesday, April 28, 2004

2:00 a.m. wake-up call. We put all of our luggage into the bus and off to the airport. Part of our group had to make a detour to Poland, first to Krakow and then Warsaw where we waited for three hours. We arrived in Toronto at 12:00 midnight European time, which was about 5:00 p.m. Toronto time.

We had a memorable trip with a great group of students.

FOR YEARS, IF ANY OF MY GRANDCHILDREN ASKED ME ABOUT THE NUMBER tattooed on my arm, I would always say, "That's my old telephone number. I put it there so I wouldn't forget it." After a while, they weren't satisfied with that anymore, and so I started to tell them little bits and pieces about World War II. When they got a little older, they starting hearing about the concentration camps from other people. I decided to come clean.

My granddaughter, Elizabeth (Lisa) Brass-Kaufman, at the age of twenty-eight, encouraged me to put my story on paper, and she started me off by typing part of this testimony. It was never my intention to write a book—I began by writing down some of my story for my grandchildren. Since then, however, especially since I started lecturing at the request of the Holocaust Educational and Memorial Centre, I have been asked many times to write about my experiences. Now Lisa is serving as a volunteer docent for the Holocaust Centre.

Dear Lisa, I thank you and your husband, David, for all the support you have given me. Love, Opa.

I also want to give a very special thank you to my daughter, Katy Englishman-Brass, and her husband, Danny, who were able to make sense out of what I had typed. I know that this was not an easy task for you to do, both physically and emotionally. I hesitated for a long time before I agreed to allow you to enter my testimony on the computer. Katy, I don't think that anyone else could have done a better job than you did. Love you, Dad.

A special thank you to computer wizard Jeff Ivers for his technical expertise.

I Family Relationships

FAMILY OF MICHAEL ENGLISHMAN

Born Michel Engelschman, February 11, 1921

Immediate Family

Engelschman, Levi	Father	born December 9, 1884	died in Auschwitz-Birkenau
Engelschman, Rachel	Mother	born October 13, 1883	died in Auschwitz-Birkenau
Buijtekant, Esther	Sister	born June 27, 1909	died in Auschwitz-Birkenau
Buijtekant, Jacob	Brother-in-law	born November 21, 1909	died in Auschwitz-Birkenau
Buijtekant, Joseph	Nephew	born December 26, 1935	died in Auschwitz-Birkenau
Engelschman, Anna	Sister	born January 9, 1911	died in Auschwitz-Birkenau
Engelschman, Duifje	Sister	born September 20, 1917	died in Auschwitz-Birkenau
Les, Henriette	Wife	born December 9, 1923	died in Auschwitz-Birkenau
Engelschman, Hendrika	Sister	born March 31, 1925	died in Auschwitz-Birkenau

Extended Family That I Found in Holland in 1995

- Louis Engelschman, my first cousin, whose father and my father were brothers, and his family
- Louis's eldest brother, Henry, and his wife and children
- Louis's brother, Ruud, and his wife and family
- Louis's brother, Wauter, and his family
- Another first cousin, Barend, and his sister, Duifje

• My first cousin Margaret Van Schaik-Ereira (Greetje), whose mother was Sara Engelschman, my father's sister

FAMILY OF HENDRIKA ENGLISHMAN
Born Hendrika Brandon, January 4, 1912

Immediate Family

Brandon, Daniel	Father	born May 6, 1882	died in Auschwitz-Birkenau
Brandon, Keetje Jacobs	Mother	born January 1, 1880	died in 1935
Pels, Marcus	Husband	born February 5, 1905	died in Auschwitz-Birkenau
Brandon, Aaron	Brother	born July 6, 1922	died in Auschwitz-Birkenau
Brass, Keetje (Katy)	Daughter	born September 14, 1938	
Englishman, Philip	Son	born August 5, 1941	

Rika's cousin, Elizabeth Van Buiten, her husband, Jan, and their children

II LIST OF PRISONS AND CONCENTRATION CAMPS I WAS IN, 1942 TO 1945

Amstelveense Weg, Amsterdam, prison

The Burght, Breda, Holland, prison

Vught, Holland, concentration camp

Auschwitz-Birkenau, Poland, concentration camp

Janina Grube coal mine, Poland, concentration camp

Buna-Monowitz, IG Farben Works, Poland, concentration camp

Dora-Nordhausen, v-1 and v-2 works, Germany, concentration camp

Liberated by U.S. troops, April 1945

Life Writing Series

In the **Life Writing Series,** Wilfrid Laurier University Press publishes life writing and new life-writing criticism in order to promote autobiographical accounts, diaries, letters, and testimonials written and/or told by women and men whose political, literary, or philosophical purposes are central to their lives. **Life Writing** features the accounts of ordinary people, written in English, or translated into English from French or the languages of the First Nations or from any of the languages of immigration to Canada. **Life Writing** will also publish original theoretical investigations about life writing, as long as they are not limited to one author or text.

Priority is given to manuscripts that provide access to those voices that have not traditionally had access to the publication process.

Manuscripts of social, cultural, and historical interest that are considered for the series, but are not published, are maintained in the **Life Writing Archive** of Wilfrid Laurier University Library.

Series Editor
Marlene Kadar
Humanities Division, York University

Manuscripts to be sent to
Brian Henderson, Director
Wilfrid Laurier University Press
75 University Avenue West
Waterloo, Ontario, Canada N2L 3C5

Books in the Life Writing Series
Published by Wilfrid Laurier University Press

Haven't Any News: Ruby's Letters from the Fifties edited by Edna Staebler with an Afterword by Marlene Kadar • 1995 / x + 165 pp. / ISBN 0-88920-248-6

"I Want to Join Your Club": Letters from Rural Children, 1900–1920 edited by Norah L. Lewis with a Preface by Neil Sutherland • 1996 / xii + 250 pp. (30 b&w photos) / ISBN 0-88920-260-5

And Peace Never Came by Elisabeth M. Raab with Historical Notes by Marlene Kadar • 1996 / x + 196 pp. (12 b&w photos, map) / ISBN 0-88920-281-8

Dear Editor and Friends: Letters from Rural Women of the North-West, 1900–1920 edited by Norah L. Lewis • 1998 / xvi + 166 pp. (20 b&w photos) / ISBN 0-88920-287-7

The Surprise of My Life: An Autobiography by Claire Drainie Taylor with a Foreword by Marlene Kadar • 1998 / xii + 268 pp. (+8 colour photos and 92 b&w photos) / ISBN 0-88920-302-4

Memoirs from Away: A New Found Land Girlhood by Helen M. Buss / Margaret Clarke • 1998 / xvi + 153 pp. / ISBN 0-88920-350-4

The Life and Letters of Annie Leake Tuttle: Working for the Best by Marilyn Färdig Whiteley • 1999 / xviii + 150 pp. / ISBN 0-88920-330-X

Marian Engel's Notebooks: "Ah, mon cahier, écoute" edited by Christl Verduyn • 1999 / viii + 576 pp. / ISBN 0-88920-333-4 cloth / ISBN 0-88920-349-0 paper

Be Good Sweet Maid: The Trials of Dorothy Joudrie by Audrey Andrews • 1999 / vi + 276 pp. / ISBN 0-88920-334-2

Working in Women's Archives: Researching Women's Private Literature and Archival Documents edited by Helen M. Buss and Marlene Kadar • 2001 / vi + 120 pp. / ISBN 0-88920-341-5

Repossessing the World: Reading Memoirs by Contemporary Women by Helen M. Buss • 2002 / xxvi + 206 pp. / ISBN 0-88920-408-X cloth / ISBN 0-88920-410-1 paper

Chasing the Comet: A Scottish-Canadian Life by Patricia Koretchuk • 2002 / xx + 244 pp. / ISBN 0-88920-407-1

The Queen of Peace Room by Magie Dominic • 2002 / xii + 115 pp. / ISBN 0-88920-417-9

China Diary: The Life of Mary Austin Endicott by Shirley Jane Endicott • 2002 / xvi + 251 pp. / ISBN 0-88920-412-8

The Curtain: Witness and Memory in Wartime Holland by Henry G. Schogt • 2003 / xii + 132 pp. / ISBN 0-88920-396-2

Teaching Places by Audrey J. Whitson • 2003 / xiii + 178 pp. / ISBN 0-88920-425-X

Through the Hitler Line by Laurence F. Wilmot, M.C. • 2003 / xvi + 152 pp. / ISBN 0-88920-448-9

Where I Come From by Vijay Agnew • 2003 / xiv + 298 pp. / ISBN 0-88920-414-4

The Water Lily Pond by Han Z. Li • 2004 / x + 254 pp. / ISBN 0-88920-431-4

The Life Writings of Mary Baker McQuesten: Victorian Matriarch edited by Mary J. Anderson • 2004 / xxii + 338 pp. / ISBN 0-88920-437-3

Seven Eggs Today: The Diaries of Mary Armstrong, 1859 and 1869 edited by Jackson W. Armstrong • 2004 / xvi + 228 pp. / ISBN 0-88920-440-3

Love and War in London: A Woman's Diary 1939–1942 by Olivia Cockett; edited by Robert W. Malcolmson • 2005 / xvi + 208 pp. / ISBN 0-88920-458-6

Incorrigible by Velma Demerson • 2004 / vi + 178 pp. / ISBN 0-88920-444-6

Auto/biography in Canada: Critical Directions edited by Julie Rak • 2005 / viii + 264 pp. ISBN 0-88920-478-0

Tracing the Autobiographical edited by Marlene Kadar, Linda Warley, Jeanne Perreault, and Susanna Egan • 2005 / viii + 280 pp. / ISBN 0-88920-476-4

Must Write: Edna Staebler's Diaries edited by Christl Verduyn • 2005 / viii + 304 pp. / ISBN 0-88920-481-0

Pursuing Giraffe: A 1950s Adventure by Anne Innis Dagg • 2006 / xvi + 284 pp. / ISBN 0-88920-463-2

Must Write: Edna Staebler's Diaries, edited by Christl Verduyn • 2005 / viii + 304 pp. / ISBN 0-88920-481-0

Food That Really Schmecks, by Edna Staebler • 2007 / xxiv + 334 pp. / ISBN 978-0-88920-521-5

163256: A Memoir of Resistance, by Michael Englishman • 2007 / xvi + 112 pp. / ISBN 978-1-55458-009-5